History Odyssey

Early Modern
level two

Kathleen Johnson

 Pandia Press

Published by
Pandia Press
Mount Dora, FL

Visit www.pandiapress.com for sample pages of Pandia Press publications and for ordering information.

Table of Contents

Table of Contents

Dear Parents and Teachers,

Your child is about to embark on a great adventure—studying the history of mankind. History Odyssey guides are intended to assist your child on this adventure with access to the greatest resources and with assistance in organizing a tremendous amount of information. This guide is written for the logic-to rhetoric-stage of a classical education (approximately sixth through tenth grade) and will challenge your child to compare and contrast, analyze, research, write, and outline. This study guide expands upon the skills taught in previous History Odyssey level two courses. Students who did not complete *Ancients (level two)* and *Middle Ages (level two)* should be able to successfully complete this course if they have some prior knowledge of outlining, research, and summarizing.

This study guide contains many writing assignments including biographies and essays. Although basic instructions are given, History Odyssey is not a writing course. We highly recommend that students complete a formal writing class prior to or during this course. An Essay Rubric Checklist is included in the worksheet section to assist you with evaluating your child's essay work.

The lesson plans in this study guide speak directly to your child for independent use. However, we recommend assisting with the first few lessons and acknowledge that some students may need assistance throughout the course. Read over the following instruction pages with your child and assist him or her in setting up a binder and gathering resources. Most of the lessons are written to be completed in one to two sittings. The exceptions to this are the lessons that instruct students to read one of the twelve literature books and those containing library research assignments. For these lessons, students should be given ample time to complete the tasks before going on to the next lesson unless otherwise indicated. If your child's interest is sparked by a subject, refer to the resource list and allow him or her to spend extra time on that subject. We suggest students at this grade level spend about two hours studying history three to four days a week. At that pace, this guide provides a one-year history course. Keep in mind that these lesson plans combine several subjects—history, reading, writing, and geography.

Most of the literature books used in this study guide are at a level that logic stage students can read independently. Some students may benefit from having the books read aloud. Students will not be interrupted with comprehension questions or vocabulary work while reading the assigned literature. We feel that interrupting the reading of these wonderful books tends to make reading laborious and frustrating. However, you might want to suggest that your child read with a pencil in hand and circle difficult words to look up later. Also it is recommended that you have discussions with your child during the reading to ensure comprehension. Ideally, you will read the books as well.

A new addition to History Odyssey is the reference to Web sites throughout this and future study guides. It is not necessary to access Web sites in order to complete this course. All Web site references provide optional resources for research. We highly recommend students not use the Web sites exclusively for their research. In today's high-tech world, it is easy for students to engage in "lazy research" by depending solely on the Internet for information. Although the Internet does contain valuable information, it also contains vast amounts of inaccurate information and harmful materials (see our disclaimer about Web sites on the copyright page). Please guide and supervise your child in Internet research and encourage him to engage in plenty of "old fashioned" library research as well.

Notes

Literature: There is a lot of good historical fiction available for reading while studying this time period. If your child has already read one or more of the books in the required reading for this course, you could substitute a similar book. See Appendix N for suggested books.

Timeline Work: In this edition of History Odyssey, students will not be given timeline dates for copying onto their timelines. Students are expected to identify significant dates themselves. Some students may require assistance at first in picking out the most important dates. Make sure that your child is not writing every date encountered on his or her timeline.

Essays: In this edition of level two History Odyssey your child will be asked to write formal essays. Prior to writing the first essay there is a short lesson, "How to Write an Essay." This lesson presents a starting point to teaching your child essay writing. (Many students may require additional instruction from a writing course that addresses essays and thesis writing. See Appendix N for recommended courses.) The lesson on essays includes instruction in writing topic sentences. Topic sentences are similar to thesis statements, which are presented in Level Three courses. This lesson recommends essays be five paragraphs in length comprised of three main ideas to support the topic sentence. Please use this as a guideline only. If the topic sentence created by your child requires only two main ideas, then by all means don't require creation of another one just to fit the model. As your child becomes a more proficient writer, allow him or her to break away from this model and be more creative with writing.

Carry On, Mr. Bowditch: This book and the subsequent lesson and map work are optional because they will significantly increase the length of this course. If time is short, we recommend your child read this wonderful book another time.

Lessons 14 and 76: These lessons require your child search through several newspaper articles. Please ensure access to several newspapers on the days of these lessons.

Lessons 21 and 79: In these lessons we recommend your child gives a presentation using PowerPoint or another presentation software if available. For examples of history presentations given with PowerPoint visit: www.pppst.com/worldhistory.HTML.

Lessons 24 and 27: These lessons involve your child looking at the horrors of the slave trade. He or she will be reading a somewhat graphic description of life aboard a slave ship and examining the reasons why people became involved in enslaving other human beings. These exercises are not attempts to justify the slave trade— quite the contrary. Assist your child in these assignments. Encourage contemplation of these questions: Why do good people sometimes do bad things? How does crowd mentality contribute? How did people involved in the slave trade justify ignoring individual rights? Please ensure that your child understands the point of these exercises. If you feel there is a chance that your child might not understand, it would be best that he skips these lessons.

Lesson 46: In this lesson your child will be constructing a book jacket and will need craft supplies. Refer to the lesson for a supply list.

Lesson 76: Prior to this lesson about Napoleon, you might want to rent the PBS mini-series *Napoleon* by director David Grubin (2000). This excellent biography is available on DVD from Netflix and PBS, and also through cable and satellite TV on demand. Use parental discretion with this video. It contains a few disturbing descriptions of war violence, and some of Napoleon's letters deserve a PG-13 rating.

Required Resources

The following resources are required to complete this course.

- ❑ **The Kingfisher History Encyclopedia* (2004 or newer edition) - **KFH**
- ❑ **The Story of Mankind* by Hendrik Willem Van Loon (optional)$^\Delta$ - **TSOM**
- ❑ **History Odyssey Timeline from Pandia Press (or a homemade timeline)*
- ❑ *I, Juan de Pareja* by Elizabeth Borton de Treviño
- ❑ *Amos Fortune: Free Man* by Elizabeth Yates
- ❑ *The Landing of the Pilgrims* by James Daugherty
- ❑ *The Witch of Blackbird Pond* by Elizabeth George Speare
- ❑ *Oliver Twist* by Charles Dickens (abridged by Puffin Classics)**
- ❑ *Kidnapped* by Robert Louis Stevenson
- ❑ *Island of the Blue Dolphins* by Scott O'Dell
- ❑ *Johnny Tremain* by Esther Forbes
- ❑ *The American Revolution* by Bruce Bliven, Jr.
- ❑ *Carry on, Mr. Bowditch* by Jean Lee Latham (optional reading)
- ❑ *The Captain's Dog: My Journey with the Lewis and Clark Tribe* by Roland Smith
- ❑ *The Sign of the Beaver* by Elizabeth George Speare

*These resources are used for all History Odyssey level two study guides.

** This edition of *Oliver Twist* is abridged for length only and contains Dickens' original words. Advanced readers, and those with more time, might want to read the unabridged *Oliver Twist*.

Δ *The Story of Mankind*: Due to the polarizing nature of this book, it is optional reading in this level two course. It should be considered a possible resource for gathering information. If students choose not to read TSOM, they might need to seek out other resources to complete some of the lessons.

Other Supplies Needed

- Three-ring binder (2-inch size is recommended)
- Six binder dividers with tabs
- Lined paper or computer paper
- A three-hole punch
- A detailed atlas or world wall map
- A ruler or straight edge
- Colored pencils
- Copies of the worksheets (see the worksheet section for number of copies required)
- Internet access
- Dictionary, encyclopedias, and library access
- Computer presentation software such as PowerPoint, Keynote, Corel Presentations, or movie-making software (optional)

Setting Up Your Binder

Divide your binder into the following six sections:

1. Summaries

2. Men & Women

3. Wars & Conflicts

4. Art, Inventions, & Architecture

5. Maps & Worksheets

6. Timeline

Insert this study guide in the front of your binder. Label the dividers and insert lined paper into the first four sections. Three-hole-punch your timeline* and place it along with the maps and worksheets in their appropriate sections.

*Alternatively, you can display your timeline on a wall while you are working on it, and then place it in your binder when finished. See the next page for information on making your own timeline.

Lesson Assignments

Throughout these lessons you will be asked to summarize readings by finding central ideas and outlining. You will also mark dates on your timeline, color and label maps, and read from the list of resources. Try to do all of the assignments listed. When asked to add a person or event to your binder, title your entry and include some important information. Place the entry in the appropriate section of your binder. A short summary is one to two sentences. A lengthy summary should be a complete paragraph consisting of at least five sentences. When you are finished with this course you will have a binder full of information you have learned and work you have completed. More importantly, you will have an education about early modern history to treasure always.

Map Work

Geography is an important part of history and you will be learning a great deal of early modern and modern day geography throughout this course. When working with a map, carefully color areas with colored pencils. Do not use markers, as they will bleed through the paper and blot out labels and other markings. You can make the land areas colorful by coloring each country or area a different pastel shade. When labeling, use a ruler to lightly make a pencil line. Print the name carefully on the line with a fine-point black pen and then erase the pencil line after your ink dries. Take your time to make the maps beautiful keepsake treasures of your time spent studying early modern history.

Outlining

In this course, you will be creating three-level outlines from readings found in the *Kingfisher History Encyclopedia*. Outlining is a very important skill to learn. If you learn this skill well it will help you tremendously when reading complicated writings, when preparing notes for oral presentations and research papers, and when taking notes in high school and college courses. Outlining will help you separate main ideas from details. It will help you break down information into the most important parts and organize them.

Timeline

You will need a timeline to complete this course. Using a timeline will assist you in organizing information and seeing connections between events. At the end of this course, you will be completing an interesting exercise in which you analyze the data on your timeline. Timelines can be purchased or constructed. To construct your own timeline you will need a piece of butcher paper about 2½ feet long. Draw a line across the paper a few inches from the top. Leaving a little space at the beginning of your line for earlier events, mark dates beginning at the year 1575. Continue marking dates in 25-year increments ending with the year 1875. Space your dates approximately 2 inches apart. Accordion-fold the timeline, three-hole-punch it, and place it in your binder.

As you enter events on the timeline you can either draw lines from the information to the point they occurred on the timeline or you can enter a reference number on the timeline that refers to a corresponding entry on a separate piece of paper.

Write events directly on your timeline:

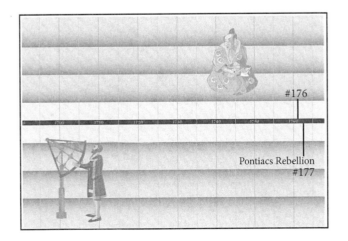

Write reference numbers on your timeline that refer to entries on separate paper.

#176 -
In 1762, Rousseau (considered the Father of the French Revolution) wrote *The Social Contract*, in which he emphasized the rights of individuals.

#177 –
1763, Pontiacs Rebellion. Native Americans resisted British settlements in America. Pontiac, tribal leader of the Ottawa, led a rebellion that killed 200 British settlers. Pontiac eventually surrendered.

Part I
Trade and Rebellion

Review of Europe and the Stuarts

GET READY   For this lesson you will need:

- Map 1, Europe
- KFH
- TSOM (optional)
- Fine-point black pen or pencil
- Colored pencils
- Atlas

☐
> On Map 1, use your atlas to label the following areas:
>
> **Water Areas:**
> Atlantic Ocean
> Mediterranean Sea
>
> **Countries:**
> England   Italy
> France   Ireland
> Spain   Scotland
> Germany   Sweden
>
> **Cities (label with a dot):**
> London   Paris
> Oxford
>
> Shade the area of Europe your favorite color.

☐ Read TSOM chapter 45, "The English revolution." This chapter begins with a review of warfare in Europe and English history that you will remember from studying the Middle Ages. Read the first eight pages of this chapter carefully to review events such as the Battle of Hastings and the Hundred Years' War, and significant people such as William Duke of Normandy, Harold of Wessex, Joan of Arc, Henry VII, Henry VIII, Philip II, Elizabeth, and the Tudors. New material begins on page 301 with the history of the Stuart Dynasty and James I.

☐ Read KFH pp. 246 - 247 "The Stuarts" and 260 - 261 "English Civil War."

☐ Add the following to the Men & Women section of your binder along with lengthy summaries containing information from TSOM and KFH:

> **The Stuarts**
> **James I**
> **Frederick**
> **Charles I**
> **Oliver Cromwell**

☐ Describe the King James Bible in the Summaries section of your binder.

☐ Add significant dates to your timeline.

The English Civil War

GET READY   For this lesson you will need:

- Worksheet: Record of War or Conflict
- KFH
- TSOM (optional)

☐ In your Summaries section, write a one-page summary defining the idea of the "divine right of kings" held by James I and Charles I. Include information on how these rulers abused their power. Also explain the English people's reaction to "divine right" and the role of Parliament. Information for this summary can be found in TSOM and KFH.

☐ Record the English Civil War using the worksheet titled "Record of War or Conflict." Include information on the Cavaliers and the Roundheads. See instructions below. (Make several copies of this worksheet; do not write on the original.)

Instructions for completing a Record of War or Conflict worksheet: When completing a worksheet for a war or conflict, use the back side of the paper if you run out of room in any of the boxes. In the "General Summary" box, write two or three sentences that summarize the war. Record all of the parties involved in the conflict in the corresponding box. In the box titled "Events Leading Up to the War or Conflict," record the events that created tension between the parties involved including legislation, condition and complaints of the people, significant individuals and their actions, disagreements, etc. In the box titled "Reasons for the Fighting," record the one or two events that triggered the actual fighting. Usually these are the events that "broke the camel's back," so to speak. In "Significant Battles and Their Outcomes," list all of the major battles with dates, who was fighting, where, and the outcome (who won). For the "Final Outcome" box, record who won the war or conflict in the end (if there was a true winner) and what they won (land, power, rights, etc.). In the box titled "Results (Future Effects)," look ahead in history and record at least one long-term effect of this war (Were the people better off? Did it create other conflicts? How did it change the nation that was conquered and the nation that won?). In "Other Information and Your Assessment," record any interesting facts not recorded elsewhere and give your assessment of this war (Was it a just war? In hindsight, could things have been done differently? Which side do you sympathize with?). Include a map sketch of the territories involved if applicable. Place the completed worksheet in the Wars & Conflicts section of your binder.

☐ Add significant dates to your timeline.

Lesson 3 — The Thirty Years' War and Religious Warfare

GET READY For this lesson you will need:

- Map 2, The Thirty Years' War (1648)
- KFH
- TSOM (optional)
- Fine-point black pen or pencil
- Atlas
- Worksheet: Record of War or Conflict

☐

> On Map 2, use your atlas to label the following:
>
> Denmark   Austria
>
> Switzerland   Sweden
>
> France   Water areas
>
> Netherlands (Holland)
>
> Prague (located in modern-day Czech Republic)

> Most of what was once called Bohemia is now called the Czech Republic. Locate the Czech Republic in your atlas and write it in parentheses on your map.

☐ Read KFH pp. 252 - 253 "The Thirty Years' War."

☐ Read TSOM chapter 44 "Religious Warfare."

☐ Summarize the Thirty Years' War in the Wars & Conflicts section of your binder using a Record of War or Conflict worksheet.

Web site: For more information on the Thirty Years' War:
· www.pipeline.com/%7Ecwa/TYWHome.htm.

☐ Record significant dates on your timeline.

Lesson 4 — France

GET READY For this lesson you will need:

- Map 3: 17th Century France
- KFH

☐ Read KFH pp. 254 - 255 "France and Richelieu."

☐ Begin a three level outline on France by outlining this reading. Include main topics, subtopics, and details in your outline. You will be adding to this outline in Lesson 5. Place all of your outlines in the Summaries section of your binder. Your outline might begin like this:

<u>Seventeenth Century France</u>

I. Louis XIII appointed Cardinal Richelieu chief minister of France in 1624.
   A. Richelieu worked to unify and strengthen France.
      1. He reduced the power of regional dukes.
      2. He squashed French Protestant Huguenots.
   B. Richelieu was disliked by many.
      1. He ended privileges of previous religious and political leaders.
      2. He increased taxes.
      3. He used force.
II. Austria and Spain were the main threats to France.
   A. Richelieu paid Sweden, Denmark and the Netherlands to fight the Hapsburgs in Germany.
   B. (Add another subtopic here.)
   C. (Add another subtopic here.)
III. When Richelieu died, Cardinal Mazarin took over.
   (Add subtopics here.)

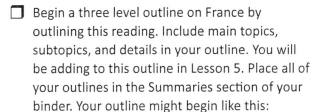

☐

> On Map 3, use your atlas to label:
> France   Spain   England
> Italy   Water areas
>
> Trace the Rhine river blue.
>
> Shade France your favorite color.
>
> Locate the Pyrenees Mountains in your atlas. Draw and label them on your map.
>
> Shade the Hapsburg Empire your second favorite color (within the dotted lines).
>
> Complete the map key.

☐ Record significant dates on your timeline.

☐ Add **Cardinal Richelieu** to your Men & Women section along with a short summary.

5 Louis XIV, The Sun King

GET READY   For this lesson you will need:

- KFH
- TSOM (optional)

☐ Read KFH p. 264 "The Sun King."

☐ Continue your outline on France by adding more topics, subtopics, and details as appropriate. Some main topics you might want to use:

IV. Louis XIV became King of France at a young age.
(add subtopics and details as appropriate)

V.   Louis XIV appointed Jean Colbert as controller-general.
(add subtopics and details as appropriate)

VII. Louis XIV became rigid in his control and lived in splendor.
(add subtopics and details as appropriate)

VIII. Louis XIV began war to expand France's borders.
(add subtopics and details as appropriate)

☐ Add the palace Versailles in the Art, Inventions, & Architecture section of your binder along with a short summary (add a sketch if you wish).

☐ Read TSOM chapter 46 "The Balance of Power."

☐ Record significant dates on your timeline.

6 Louis XIV, The Sun King (cont.)

GET READY   For this lesson you will need:

- Appendix A: Attribution of Sources
- Appendix B: How to Write a Biography
- Encyclopedias, library access, and/or Internet access

☐ Read Appendix A, "Attribution of Sources," which explains how to properly credit a resource.

☐ Write a biography on Louis XIV. Your biographies for this course should be one to three pages long. Begin with information from your course readings and then do research (encyclopedias, library, and Internet searches) to gather more information. When writing biographies, use at least two print sources in your research. See Appendix B for information on how to write a biography. Include a bibliography at the end of your biography, listing the sources you used for your report as instructed in Appendix A. File the biographies for this course in your Men & Women section.

Helpful Web site:
- www.louis-xiv.de/index.php?t=start&a=start.

·

7 I, Juan de Pareja

GET READY   For this lesson you will need:

- *I, Juan de Pareja* by Elizabeth Borton de Trevino

☐ Begin reading *I, Juan de Pareja*. Continue with your history lessons while reading but complete your reading before Lesson 10, where you will be given an art assignment.

Spain

GET READY   For this lesson you will need:

- Map 4, Spain
- Colored pencils
- Fine-point black pen or pencil
- Atlas
- KFH

☐ On Map 4, use your atlas to label the following countries and some of the cities mentioned in *I, Juan de Pareja*:

Spain	Africa	Italy
Sardinia	France	Portugal
Sicily	Genoa	Seville
Naples	Barcelona	Madrid

Label water areas.

Shade the country of Spain your favorite color.

☐ Read KFH pp. 256 - 257 "Decline of Spain."

☐ Add the following to your Men & Women section along with short summaries:

Philip III   **Philip IV**

Charles II (add more in the next lesson)

Philip V (Philip of Anjou) (add more in the next lesson)

☐ Record significant dates on your timeline.

Spanish Succession

GET READY   For this lesson you will need:

- KFH
- Worksheet: Record of War or Conflict
- Map 4, Spain
- Colored pencils
- Fine-point black pen or pencil

☐ Read KFH p. 279 "The Spanish Succession."

☐ Record the Spanish Succession on a Record of War and Conflict worksheet.

☐ Add to the summaries of **Charles II** and **Philip of Anjou** in your Men & Women section.

☐ On Map 4, use KFH p. 279 to label the following:

Germany	Austria	England
Savoy	Gibraltar	Vienna
Utrecht	Spanish Netherlands	

Draw and shade the boundaries of land distribution.

Complete the map key.

17th Century Art and Architecture

GET READY   For this lesson you will need:
- *I, Juan de Pareja*
- KFH
- Encyclopedias, library access, art history books, and/or Internet access

☐ Finish reading *I, Juan de Pareja*.

☐ Read KFH pp. 282-285 "The Arts 1601 - 1707."

☐ In the Art, Inventions, & Architecture section of your binder record short summaries about **Christopher Wren**, Baroque style, and the Great Fire of London.

☐ Choose three artists from 17th century Baroque style and create an art gallery page for each one in the Art, Inventions, & Architecture section of your binder. At the top of each page write a few sentences on the life and work of the artist. Below the biography paste images of his artwork. Images can be copied or scanned from art books; copied, pasted, and printed from Internet sites; or found in art sticker books.

A few helpful web sites:

· www.artcyclopedia.com/artists/velazquez_diego.html (links to paintings by Velázquez)

· www.artcyclopedia.com/artists/juan_de_pareja.html (links to paintings by Juan de Pareja)

· www.ibiblio.org/wm/paint/auth (biographies and paintings by many artists such as Rubens, Rembrandt, Velázquez, Caravaggio, and Van Dyck)

Scientific Revolution or the Age of Reason

GET READY For this lesson you will need:
- KFH
- Dictionary and/or encyclopedia

☐ Read KFH pp. 268 - 269 "The Age of Reason" and 286-287 "Science and Technology 1601 - 1707."

☐ Add the following to the Men & Women section or the Art, Inventions, & Architecture section of your binder along with short summaries:

John Locke (save room to add more later)
Jethro Tull (save room to add more later)

Sir Isaac Newton	**Robert Boyle**
Anders Celcius	**Leibniz**
Kepler	**René Descartes**
Tycho Brahe	**Galileo Galilei**
Francis Bacon	**Carl Linnaeus**

☐ Summarize the Age of Reason in the Summaries section of your binder. Include in your summary a detailed definition of scientific method from a dictionary or encyclopedia.

☐ Add short summaries about the Royal Observatory, the telescope, and other inventions you read about in KFH to the Art, Inventions, & Architecture section of your binder along with sketches.

Scientific Revolution (cont.)

GET READY For this lesson you will need:
- KFH
- Encyclopedias, library access, art history books, and/or Internet access

☐ Choose one of the men from the last lesson and write a one- to three-page biography. Use at least two print sources in your research and don't forget to include a bibliography. Place your biography in the Men & Women section or Art, Inventions, & Architecture section of your binder.

Evaluating Resources

GET READY For this lesson you will need:
- TSOM (optional)
- Appendix C: Guidelines for Evaluating Sources in History
- Worksheet: Evaluating Sources in History

During your study of history you will encounter many different sources describing events and people from the past. All of these accounts will be biased (prejudiced) in one way or another! All historic documents and reports reflect the author's point of view. Even accounts that appear to be mostly a list of facts can be biased by which facts are reported and which are omitted. This is not necessarily a bad thing. Some of the more interesting accounts to read are those that clearly take a stand and express an opinion. In high school and college you will write persuasive thesis papers in which you will state and then defend an opinion.

It is important, however, to be able to evaluate accounts and consider the source by understanding the position of the author and his or her intention. It is also very important to seek out several resources from differing points of view and not depend on only one source.

It is easier to detect an author's prejudice in some accounts of history than in others. Reports marked as "opinion" or "commentary" are the easiest; other accounts are more difficult. Many of the readings in TSOM, for example, represent persuasive writing—the author is presenting facts in a way that is attempting to get you to feel a certain way and convince you of something. You will begin learning how to evaluate sources with a reading in TSOM.

☐ Read TSOM chapter 60 "The Age Science." If you are not using TSOM, locate an article online concerning The Age of Science. One suggestion:
· www.scienceandyou.org/articles/ess_18.shtml

☐ Read Appendix C, "Guidelines for Evaluating Sources in History."

☐ Complete the worksheet titled Evaluating Sources in History using the reading in TSOM. (Make several copies of this worksheet for future lessons before marking the original.) Place the completed worksheet in the Summaries section of your binder.

14 Evaluating Resources (cont.)

GET READY For this lesson you will need:

- Newspapers, news magazines, television news, and/or Internet news reports
- Worksheet: Evaluating Sources in History (2)

☐ Gather articles from your local newspapers or from news magazines. Locate two or more articles on the same topic but from differing points of view. For example, you could find an article about a political issue written by someone who appears to oppose the issue and an article written by someone who appears to support it. If you cannot find print articles from differing points of view, you could substitute a television or Internet news report for one or both of the articles. Avoid articles identified as commentaries or opinion. Try to find reports that on the surface appear to be factual reports and are presented as informational news. For the purpose of this exercise, choose only secondary sources. For each article, complete an "Evaluating Sources in History" worksheet. Attach the articles to the worksheets and place the completed worksheets in the Summaries section of your binder.

15 Galileo

GET READY For this lesson you will need:

- Appendix D: The Crimes of Galileo
- Worksheet: Evaluating Sources in History (2)

☐ Read The Crimes of Galileo in Appendix D ("The Indictment of Galileo" and "Galileo's Abjuration"). (*Indictment* and *abjuration* are common legal terms. Look them up in a dictionary if you do not know their meanings.)

☐ Complete two copies of the Evaluating Sources worksheet—one for the indictment and one for the abjuration. Place the completed worksheets in the Summaries section of your binder.

16 Early American Settlers

GET READY For this lesson you will need:

- KFH
- Map 5, Early North American Settlements
- Fine-point black pen or pencil

☐ Read KFH pp. 248 - 249 "Early American Settlers."

☐ Create a three-level outline of this reading. Remember to include main topics, subtopics, and details.

☐
> On Map 5, refer to KFH p. 248 to label the following:
>
> | | |
> |---|---|
> | Louisiana | Plymouth |
> | Hudson Bay | Canada |
> | Quebec | Gulf of Mexico |
> | Virginia | Jamestown |
> | Great Lakes | New Amsterdam |
> | Gulf of St. Lawrence | (New York) |
> | Montreal | |

☐ Add **John Rolfe** and the **Pilgrims** to your Men & Women section along with short summaries.

☐ Record significant dates on your timeline.

17 *The Landing of the Pilgrims*

GET READY For this lesson you will need:

- *The Landing of the Pilgrims* by James Daugherty
- Map 5, Early North American Settlements
- Colored pencils
- Fine-point black pen or pencil

☐ Read *The Landing of the Pilgrims*. Complete reading this book before going on to the next lesson.

☐
> As you read, draw the route of the Pilgrims beginning in London and ending at their final destination in America on Map 5 with a colored pencil. Label England, London, Holland (Netherlands), and Amsterdam. Complete the map key.

As you read add the following to your Men & Women section along with short summaries:

William Bradford	**King James**
Robert Coppin	**William Brewster**
Captain Miles Standish	**Samoset**
The Separatists	**Chief Massasoit**
John Carver	**Squanto**
Hobomok	**Witawamat**
Captain Christopher Jones	

Lesson 18 The Mayflower Compact

GET READY   For this lesson you will need:

- *The Landing of the Pilgrims*
- Dictionary and/or Internet access

The Mayflower Compact of 1620 was the first American document to describe government as an agreement among people. It was an early example of American democracy.

"In making this compact, the Pilgrims drew upon two strong traditions. One was the notion of a social contract, which dated back to biblical times. The other was the belief in covenants. Puritans believed that covenants existed not only between God and man, but also between man and man. The Mayflower Compact is such a covenant in that the settlers agreed to form a government and be bound by its rules.

"The Compact is often described as America's first constitution, but it is not a constitution in the sense of being a fundamental framework of government. Its importance lies in the belief that government is a form of covenant, and that for government to be legitimate, it must derive from the consent of the governed."

—U.S. Department of State

Look up *democracy* and write a detailed definition in your Summaries section.

Review the Mayflower Compact on pages 44-45 in *The Landing of the Pilgrims*. Find the parts of the Compact that support democracy and copy them onto the page where you defined *democracy*. How did the Compact set up a democracy for the Pilgrims? What democratic events followed the Compact in the Virginia

colony? Did the Compact declare the Pilgrims free from England? Summarize the Mayflower Compact and its effects by answering these questions in your Summaries section. Also explain what is meant by "government is a form of covenant, and that for government to be legitimate, it must derive from the consent of the governed."

Challenge: The United States government is a *representative* democracy not a *direct* democracy. Research what this means and write a summary.

Lesson 19 How to Write an Essay

GET READY   For this lesson you will need:

- Appendix E: How to Write an Essay
- *The Landing of the Pilgrims*
- Worksheet: Essay Worksheet
- Worksheet: Essay Rubric Checklist

Read Appendix E, "How to Write an Essay."

Write an essay describing how religious beliefs played a role in the journey and decisions of the Pilgrims. First create a topic sentence stating that religion played a role. To support your topic sentence, find three or more instances from *The Landing of the Pilgrims* where the Pilgrim's religious beliefs directly affected their decisions. Each instance should be a paragraph in your essay. To support your topic sentence it might be helpful to describe how the decisions might have been different if the Pilgrims had not had deep religious convictions. Begin with an outline and then write your essay from your outline as described in "How to Write an Essay." Use the Essay Worksheet and Essay Rubric Checklist to structure and improve your essay. Place a final copy of the essay in the Summaries section of your binder.

Lesson 20 India

GET READY For this lesson you will need:
- KFH
- Map 6, India
- Fine-point black pen or pencil
- Atlas

☐ Read KFH p. 265 "Decline of Mogul India" and pp. 298 - 299 "India in Transition."

☐ Create a three-level outline on India's history from 1600-1850 from your readings in KFH. Include information about the rise and fall of the Mogul Empire, the British in India, and the East India Trading Companies.

> On Map 6, use your atlas and the map on KFH p. 298 to label:
>
> | | |
> |---|---|
> | India | Pakistan (modern-day) |
> | Delhi | Ceylon (Sri Lanka) |
> | Madras | Arabian Sea |
> | Bay of Bengal | |

☐ Add the Taj Mahal to the Art, Inventions, & Architecture section of your binder along with a short summary and sketch.

☐ Add **Akbar** and **Aurangzeb** to your Men & Women section along with short summaries.

☐ Add significant dates to your timeline.

Lesson 21 East India Trading Companies

GET READY For this lesson you will need:
- KFH
- Map 7, East India Trading Companies
- Fine-point black pen or pencil
- Atlas

In the 17th century the Dutch (from the Netherlands), the English, and the French competed with each other for the trade (mostly spices) in Indonesia and India. They formed powerful organizations called the East India Companies.

☐ Read KFH p. 258 "East India Trading Companies" and p. 259 "The Dutch Empire."

☐ Record a few dates on your timeline.

> On Map 7, use your atlas to label the following:
>
> | | |
> |---|---|
> | India | London |
> | Portugal | The Netherlands (Holland) |
> | Japan | Africa |
> | France | Atlantic Ocean |
> | England | Spice Islands (Indonesia) |
> | Bombay | Philippines |
> | Indian Ocean | |
>
> Draw at least three trade routes on your map as described in KFH. For example, draw the trade route taken by the Dutch from Holland to the Cape of Good Hope to the East Indies and back again.

☐ Choose one of the following assignments:

1. Summarize the East India Companies in your Summaries section. Write a general summary describing the purpose of the East India Companies. Summarize the Dutch, English, and French East India Companies. Record the locations where they controlled trade, what they traded, and dates.

2. Create a presentation on the history of the East India Trading Companies using presentation software such as PowerPoint, Keynote, or Corel Presentations. Use charts, maps, pictures, and other effects in your presentation.

Two Web sites that do a wonderful job of presenting the story of the East India Trading Companies and provide many images for your presentation:
- www.footmarkmedia.co.uk/bltp/main.htm
- www.bl.uk/learning/histcitizen/trading/tradingplaces.html

Lesson 22 Amos Fortune: Free Man

GET READY For this lesson you will need:
- *Amos Fortune: Free Man* by Elizabeth Yates

☐ Begin reading *Amos Fortune: Free Man* by Elizabeth Yates. This biography is based on primary source documents written by Amos Fortune himself. Continue with your lessons while reading this book. Complete your reading before Lesson 27.

Lesson 23 — African States

GET READY   For this lesson you will need:

- KFH
- Map 8, Africa and the Slave Trade, 16th to 19th Centuries
- Fine-point black pen or pencil
- Colored pencils
- Atlas

☐ Read KFH pp. 272 - 273 "African States."

☐ Create a three-level outline of this reading.

☐
> On Map 8, look in your atlas and on p. 272 of KFH to label Africa and the African states of Oyo, Benin, Ethiopia, and Ashanti. Are these the modern-day names of these historic African states?
>
> Also label the Atlantic Ocean, North America, and Portugal.
>
> Draw a route from Africa to the Americas and label it "The Middle Passage."
>
> Complete the map key identifying the Middle Passage. Shade Africa your second favorite color.

☐ Add significant dates to your timeline.

Lesson 24 — African States (cont.)

GET READY   For this lesson you will need:

- Appendix F: Firsthand Account of the Slave Trade
- Worksheet: Evaluating Sources

☐ Read "Firsthand Account of the Slave Trade" found in Appendix F.

☐ Complete a copy of the "Evaluating Sources" worksheet. Place the completed worksheet in the Summaries section of your binder.

Lesson 25 — Trade and Pirates

GET READY   For this lesson you will need:

- KFH
- Map 8, Africa and the Slave Trade, 16th to 19th Centuries
- Fine-point black pen or pencil
- Colored pencils
- Atlas

☐ Read KFH pp. 270 - 271 "Slavery and Pirates."

☐
> On Map 8, label South America, the West Indies, the Caribbean Sea, Jamaica, and Europe. Draw the slave triangle as represented in KFH on p. 270. Complete the map key.

☐ Add the following to your Men & Women section along with short summaries:

   Francis Drake

   Captain Kidd

   Edward Teach (Blackbeard)

   Captain Henry Morgan

☐ Add significant dates to your timeline.

Lesson 26 — Mercantilism and Trade

GET READY   For this lesson you will need:

- TSOM (optional)
- Internet access
- *Amos Fortune: Free Man*

During the 17th and 18th centuries, England was engaged in a type of economic policy called mercantilism—the idea that a country's power depended on its wealth, and a country's wealth depended upon a favorable balance of trade—selling more goods to other countries than it bought (i.e. more exports than imports). If England earned more than it spent, then that equaled profits. England imposed Navigation Acts upon the colonists to control trade. Basically the colonies would supply England, and only England, raw products such as tobacco, sugar, and indigo. Triangle trade routes were set up to support mercantilism including the triangle for the trading of slaves that you read about in the last lesson.

☐ Read TSOM chapter 50 "The Mercantile System."

☐ **If you have access to the Internet, read more about Mercantilism at these sites:**

· score.rims.k12.ca.us/score_lessons/market_to_ market/pages/mercantilism_imports_and_e.htm

· www.sparknotes.com/testprep/books/sat2/history/ chapter5section4.rhtml

☐ Choose between these two assignments:

1. Write a one- to two-page summary on mercantilism in the summary section of your binder. Define mercantilism and include information on how England used the raw materials provided by the American colonies to increase their wealth. Explain how England's use of laws and tariffs controlled trade with the colonists. How do you think mercantilism both helped and hindered America?

2. Give a presentation on the effects of mercantilism and trade. Explain verbally and visually how mercantilism worked. Recruit volunteers to play the parts of the colonists, the English, the Africans, and others. Show the English imposing Navigation Acts and tariffs upon the colonists and demonstrate how the English made a profit. As part of your oral report, act out a trade triangle. Use props with your presentation and gather an audience. You might want to take pictures of your play presentation to put in the Summaries section of your binder.

A few common trade triangles in the 17th and 18th centuries:

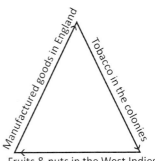
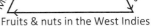
Fruits & nuts in the West Indies

Manufactured goods in England

☐ Challenge: Research and write a summary about free trade (a philosophy of trade practiced today) and describe how it differs from mercantilism.

☐ Finish reading *Amos Fortune: Free Man* before the next lesson.

Mercantilism and Trade (cont.)

GET READY For this lesson you will need:

· *Amos Fortune: Free Man*

☐ Use the information you learned from *Amos Fortune: Free Man* and from the last few lessons to write a fictitious letter to a friend about the slave trade. Pretend you are either a European ship owner who has just purchased slaves for transport to the West Indies, or an American plantation owner who has just purchased slaves at a slave market. In the letter, justify your decision to partake in the slave trade. How will you profit? Where will the slaves go and for what will they be used? Was it an easy decision? Do you care for the well-being of the slaves? What events are happening that contributed to your decision to sell or buy slaves?

☐ Write a response back as the friend to the European ship owner or plantation owner criticizing the decision to participate in the slave trade. What could he have done differently? Why was purchasing or buying slaves a wrong decision? What are some alternatives to work and profits gained through slavery? Why are the rights of individuals more important than the potential profits of slavery?

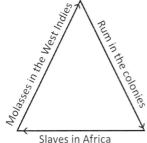
Slaves in Africa

Japan Isolates Itself from Trade

GET READY   For this lesson you will need:

- KFH
- Map 9, 17th and 18th Century Japan
- Fine-point black pen or pencil
- Colored pencils
- Atlas

☐   Read KFH pp. 244 - 245 "Japan in Isolation" and pp. 314 - 315 "Japan and Southeast Asia."

☐   Create a three-level outline title "Japan in Isolation" on both of these readings. In your outline include definitions and information about shoguns, diamyos, sumo wrestling, and Tokugawa rule, and describe how Japan both benefitted from and was hindered by isolation.

☐
> On Map 9, use KFH page 244 to label the cities of Edo, Nagasaki, Deshima, and Kyoto. Have the modern-day names of these cities changed? If so, write the new names in parentheses. Use your atlas to label the four major islands of Japan. Also label the North Pacific Ocean and the Sea of Japan. Color Japan.

☐   Record **Tokugawa Ieyasu** and **Yoshimune** in your Men & Women section along with short summaries.

☐   Add significant dates to your timeline.

Trade and Opium in China

GET READY   For this lesson you will need:

- KFH
- Worksheet: Record of War or Conflict
- Map 10, Qing Dynasty in China
- Fine-point black pen or pencil
- Colored pencils
- Atlas

During this lesson you will be outlining several readings in KFH on China. You might need to spread this lesson out over two days.

☐   Read KFH pp. 262 - 263 "China: The Qing Dynasty."

☐   Begin an outline titled "China 1650 -1850" that will include three main topics. For this reading create the first main topic about the Qing Dynasty established by the ruthless Manchu. Include several subtopics and details.

☐   Read KFH pp. 304 - 305 "Trade with China."

☐   Add to your outline on China by creating a second main topic concerning opium trade in China and the Qing Dynasty's efforts to thwart trade. Include several subtopics and details.

☐   Read KFH pp. 344 - 345 "The Opium Wars."

☐   Complete your outline on China by adding a third and final main topic about the opium wars. Include several subtopics and details.

☐   Complete a "Record of War or Conflict" worksheet on the Opium Wars.

☐
> On Map 10, shade the extent of the Qing dynasty in 1760 (within the dotted lines).
>
> Use KFH page 304 to label the following:
>
> | | |
> |---|---|
> | Guangzhou | Hong Kong |
> | Macao | Beijing |
> | Mongolia | Manchuria |
> | Siam | Laos |
> | Tibet | Turkestan |
> | China | Burma |
> | Korea | |
>
> Look on your atlas to see if the names of these areas have changed.
>
> Label the Bay of Bengal, the South China Sea, and the East China Sea.
>
> Complete the map key.

☐   Add significant dates to your timeline.

30 *The Witch of Blackbird Pond*

GET READY For this lesson you will need:

- *The Witch of Blackbird Pond* by Elizabeth George Speare
- Atlas

☐ Begin reading *The Witch of Blackbird Pond*. Continue with lessons while you read. Complete your reading by Lesson 33.

☐ After reading a few chapters, locate America, the Atlantic Ocean, and Barbados in your atlas. Trace with your finger the route made by the *Dolphin*, the colonial trading ship that brought Kit to America.

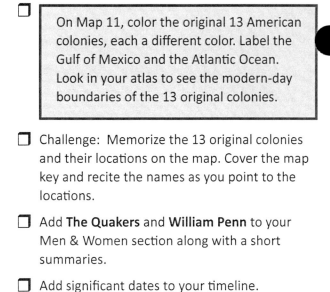

☐ On Map 11, color the original 13 American colonies, each a different color. Label the Gulf of Mexico and the Atlantic Ocean. Look in your atlas to see the modern-day boundaries of the 13 original colonies.

☐ Challenge: Memorize the 13 original colonies and their locations on the map. Cover the map key and recite the names as you point to the locations.

☐ Add **The Quakers** and **William Penn** to your Men & Women section along with a short summaries.

☐ Add significant dates to your timeline.

31 Colonial America

GET READY For this lesson you will need:

- KFH
- Encyclopedias and/or Internet access
- Map 11, Colonial America
- Fine-point black pen or pencil
- Colored pencils
- Atlas

☐ Read KFH pp. 280 - 281 "Colonial America."

☐ Choose one of the colonies mentioned in KFH to research and compose a lengthy summary (two to three paragraphs). Place your work in the Summaries section of your binder. (Choose one in which you currently live or to which you have ties.)

A few helpful Web sites:

- www.socialstudiesforkids.com/articles/ushistory/13colonies1.htm (general information on the 13 original colonies)
- www.timepage.org/spl/13colony.html (general information on the 13 original colonies)
- www.flmnh.ufl.edu/staugustine (colonial Florida)
- www.usahistory.info/southern/ (history of the southern colonies)
- www.usahistory.info/colonies/ (history of the middle colonies)

32 Colonial America (cont.)

GET READY For this lesson you will need:

- Encyclopedias, Internet, and/or library access

☐ Research an occupation from Colonial America and give an oral report. Choose from the following occupations:

Apothecary	Saddler
Founder	Printer & Binder
Carpenter	Cabinetmaker
Brickmaker	Blacksmith
Milliner	Shoemaker
Foodways	Weaver
Cooper	Silversmith
Gunsmith	Wheelwright
Basketmaker	Tailor
Wigmaker	Rural Trade Craftsman

Information about these colonial trades can be found at Colonial Williamsburg, located in Williamsburg, Virginia. If you cannot take a field trip to visit Williamsburg (very highly recommended) then visiting this Web site is the next best thing:

- www.history.org/Almanack/life/trades/tradehdr.cfm.

When preparing for an oral report, organize the information you gather in the form of an outline. Use your outline to guide your oral report. Do not read directly from your notes. To make your oral report more interesting, consider dressing the part of the occupation on which you are reporting or use visual aids like props and pictures of clothing or tools used. Have a picture taken of you giving your report and place it in your binder along with your outline.

Lesson 33 — The Salem Witch Trials

GET READY For this lesson you will need:

- *The Witch of Blackbird Pond*
- Encyclopedias, Internet, and/or library access

☐ Complete reading *The Witch of Blackbird Pond.*

☐ **If you have access to the Internet, read the primary source documents and watch a short movie about the Salem witch trials:**

- http://school.discoveryeducation.com/ schooladventures/salemwitchtrials/story/story.html

☐ Choose one of these two writing assignments:

1. Write an essay explaining the cause(s) of the Puritans' witch hysteria. Develop a specific topic sentence related to witchcraft hysteria. Don't forget to include an introduction and a conclusion. Consider these questions when writing your essay: How did Puritan culture contribute? How was the witch hysteria used to control people and justify the need for the church? Were people looking for a way to explain the unexplainable? How did the Puritans' reluctance to accept differences and anti-Quaker bigotry contribute?

2. Write an essay contrasting the Puritan legal system to our legal system today. Develop a topic sentence that describes these two systems as different. Don't forget to include an introduction and a conclusion. Consider these questions when writing your essay: Were the accused innocent until proven guilty in the Puritan legal system? How did the handling of evidence, types of evidence, and level of proof needed to convict differ from our system today? How was the accused's defense handled differently?

Lesson 34 — Russian Expansion

GET READY For this lesson you will need:

- KFH
- TSOM (optional)
- Map 12, 18th Century Russia
- Fine-point black pen or pencil
- Colored pencils
- Atlas

☐

> On Map 12, use your atlas to label the following:
>
> | | |
> |---|---|
> | Russia | Caspian Sea |
> | China | Italy |
> | Finland | Arctic Ocean |
> | Black Sea | Norway |
> | Red Sea | Germany |
> | Pacific Ocean | Mediterranean Sea |
> | Sweden | Persian Gulf |
> | Poland | Korea |
> | Baltic Sea | |
>
> Shade the expansion of Russia and complete the map key.

☐ Read TSOM chapter 47 "The Rise Russia."

☐ Read TSOM chapter 48 "Russia vs. Sweden."

☐ Read KFH pp. 276 - 277 "Russian Expansion."

☐ Add significant dates to your timeline.

Lesson 35 — Peter the Great

GET READY For this lesson you will need:

- Encyclopedias, Internet, and/or library access

☐ Write a one- to two-page biography on Peter the Great. Include in your biography information on how Peter the Great benefitted Russia, bringing it out of the Middle Ages. But also include information on how his rule as a dictator hindered Russians, especially the impoverished peasants. Use at least two print sources during your research and don't forget to include a bibliography. Place your biography in the Men & Women section of your binder.

An informative Web site:
- www.historylearningsite.co.uk/peter_the_great.htm

Sweden
Lesson 36

GET READY   For this lesson you will need:

- KFH
- Map 13, The Swedish Empire
- Atlas
- Fine-point black pen or pencil

> On Map 13, use your atlas to label the following:
>
> | | |
> |---|---|
> | England | Poland |
> | Baltic Sea | Finland |
> | North Sea | Estonia |
> | Lapland | Denmark |
> | Russia | Norway |
> | Holland (the Netherlands) | |
>
> Also label these cities:
> Stockholm
> Copenhagen
> St. Petersburg

☐ Read KFH pp. 250 - 251 "The Swedish Empire."

☐ Outline this reading.

☐ Add **Gustavus Adolphus** to your Men & Women section along with a short summary.

☐ Add significant dates to your timeline.

The Great Northern War
Lesson 37

GET READY   For this lesson you will need:

- KFH
- Worksheet: Record of War or Conflict
- Map 13, The Swedish Empire
- Colored pencils
- Fine-point black pen or pencil

☐ Read KFH p. 278 "The Great Northern War."

☐
> On Map 13, draw the boundaries and shade the Swedish Empire in 1660 as indicated in KFH. Complete the map key.

☐ Summarize the Great Northern War by completing a "Record of War or Conflict" worksheet. Place the completed worksheet in the Wars & Conflicts section of your binder.

☐ Add **Charles XII** to your Men & Women section.

☐ Add significant dates to your timeline.

Trade and Rebellion Around the World
Lesson 38

GET READY   For this lesson you will need:

- Worksheet: Trade and Rebellion Around the World
- Colored pencils

☐ Locate the worksheet titled "Trade and Rebellion Around the World." In each box on the map, write one or two major events that occurred during this time in that region of the world. Also include names of significant inventors, artists, scientists, leaders, and writers. Use information from the readings, writing assignments, and timeline entries you have completed in this course so far. Draw a line from each box to its appropriate place on the map. Color the map and place it in your Summaries section.

Part II
Revolution

What Is a Revolution?

GET READY For this lesson you will need:

- Worksheet: Revolution
- Dictionaries, encyclopedias, and/or Internet
- *Oliver Twist* by Charles Dickens

You probably have heard the word *revolution* to describe one object circling another. For example, the earth makes one revolution around the sun each year. This original definition of the word derives from the Latin *revolveree,* meaning "to turn." But the word revolution has another definition, one that has political and social meanings. This other definition of revolution came in connection with Copernicus. In his landmark thesis, *On the Revolution of the Celestial Spheres,* Copernicus "overthrew" the idea that the earth was the center of the universe as many believed at that time. His idea that the sun was the center of the universe was *revolutionary*.

☐ Look up **political/social** definitions of *revolution* from three different sources: dictionaries, encyclopedias, and/or the Internet. Try to find definitions that are detailed and somewhat different from each other. Write these definitions on the Revolution worksheet. Make several copies of this worksheet for future lessons. (It is best to make copies of the worksheet *after* you write the definitions to avoid having to rewrite them each time.)

☐ Begin reading *Oliver Twist.* Continue with your lessons while you read but finish reading before Lesson 44.

The Agricultural Revolution

GET READY For this lesson you will need:

- KFH
- Worksheet: Agricultural Revolution Web
- Worksheet: Revolution

☐ Read KFH pp. 294 - 295 "Agricultural Revolution."

☐ On the Agricultural Revolution Web worksheet, fill in the circles on the web to describe the Agricultural Revolution. Use the completed web to write a one-paragraph summary about the Agricultural Revolution. Describe what it was, where it took place, how and why it started, who was involved, who it affected, and some of the advances and setbacks it caused.

☐ Complete one copy of the "Revolution" worksheet for the Agricultural Revolution. Does the Agricultural Revolution match one or more of your definitions of a revolution? If so, circle or highlight the definition(s) it matches. Complete the worksheet by writing examples of specific circumstances that were happening for the Agricultural Revolution to take place.

☐ Add the following to the Art, Inventions, & Architecture section of your binder along with short summaries of their inventions and contributions to agriculture. Add sketches of their inventions if appropriate:

> **Thomas William Coke**
> **Lord Townshend**
> **Jethro Tull** (expand upon the entry in your Men & Women section)

☐ Add significant dates to your timeline.

The Industrial Revolution

GET READY For this lesson you will need:

- KFH
- TSOM (optional)
- Worksheet: Industrial Revolution Web

In this lesson you will read several different readings on the Industrial Revolution. Take notes as you read because you will be asked to write an essay about the Industrial Revolution in Lesson 44 based on your reading and research.

☐ Read KFH pp. 296 - 297 "Industry: Early Revolution."

☐ Read KFH p. 327 "Unrest in Britain."

☐ Read TSOM chapters 57 "The Age of the Engine" and 58 "The Social Revolution."

☐ Read KFH pp. 340 - 341 "Industrial Revolution."

☐ Complete the "Industrial Revolution Web" worksheet.

Industrial Revolution (cont.)

GET READY   For this lesson you will need:

- Worksheet: Revolution
- Colored pencils

☐ Record the inventions of the Industrial Revolution you read about in the last lesson in the Art, Inventions, & Architecture section of your binder along with short summaries. Add sketches of the inventions where appropriate.

☐ Add the dates of inventions to your timeline.

☐ Complete one copy of the "Revolution" worksheet for the Industrial Revolution. Does the Industrial Revolution match one or more of your definitions of a revolution? If so, circle or highlight the definition(s) it matches. Complete the worksheet by writing examples of specific circumstances that were happening for the Industrial Revolution to take place.

Industrial Revolution (cont.)

GET READY   For this lesson you will need:

- Encyclopedias, library, and/or Internet access

☐ Research the Industrial Revolution at your library and/or on the Internet in order to complete the writing assignment in the next lesson. When researching, focus on one of the following topics:

- Exploitation of children
- Social changes created by the revolution
- Britain's role as the "workshop of the world"
- The role of the steam engine
- The effect on farming
- Working conditions
- Growth of cities

Use at least two print sources in your research. A list of books about the Industrial Revolution can be found in Appendix N.

A few informative Web sites:

- www.history.com/topics/industrial-revolution
- www.nettlesworth.durham.sch.uk/34771
- http://americanhistory.about.com/od/industrialrev/a/indrevoverview.htm
- http://www.workhouses.org.uk

Industrial Revolution (cont.)

GET READY   For this lesson you will need:

- *Oliver Twist*
- Worksheet: Essay Worksheet
- Worksheet: Essay Rubric Checklist

☐ Complete reading *Oliver Twist*.

☐ Write an essay on the Industrial Revolution. In order to keep your essay within five paragraphs, focus on the topic that you chose in the former lesson. The Industrial Revolution was one of the most significant events in world history, and entire books have been written about it. Therefore it is important that you organize your essay around one major topic and not try to write about every aspect.

Use the information you learned while researching, while completing the "Industrial Revolution Web" worksheet, from reading *Oliver Twist*, and while completing the "Revolution" worksheet to write your essay. Make your topic sentence specific to the topic you researched. For example, if you chose "Exploitation of Children" then a possible topic sentence is: Exploitation of children in workhouses was all too common during the Industrial Revolution. Include a bibliography with your essay. Use the Essay worksheet and Essay Rubric Checklist to formulate and improve your writing. Remember to have your essay checked for grammar and spelling and place the final draft in the Summaries section of your binder.

Scottish Rebellion

GET READY For this lesson you will need:

- Map 14, Great Britain, 18th Century
- Atlas
- Fine-point black pen or pencil
- Colored pencils
- KFH
- Worksheet: Record of War or Conflict

> On Map 14, use your atlas to label the following:
>
> | | |
> |---|---|
> | Scotland | Edinburgh |
> | England | London |
> | Wales | Atlantic Ocean |
> | Ireland | North Sea. |
>
> Shade Scotland, England, and Ireland different colors.
>
> Today England, Scotland, and only a portion of Northern Ireland make up Great Britain.

☐ Read KFH p. 293 "Scotland: The Jacobites."

☐ Summarize the Scottish Rebellions by completing a "Record of War or Conflict" worksheet. Place the completed worksheet in the Wars & Conflicts section of your binder. Include information on how the English repressed the Scottish people and why the Scots rebelled.

☐ Add significant dates to your timeline.

Kidnapped

GET READY For this lesson you will need:

- *Kidnapped* by Robert Louis Stevenson
- One sheet of construction paper 11″ x 17″
- Scissors
- Ruler
- Glue stick
- Color pencils, markers, pastels, and/or paints
- Tape
- Clear contact paper (optional)
- Worksheet: Book Jacket Templates

Before reading *Kidnapped* you will begin to create a book jacket for this book. On the book jacket you will create an introduction about the historic setting of the novel, information about the author, a summary of the story, a spine, and a decorative front cover. Today you will create a description of the historic setting and a short biography of Robert Louis Stevenson. You will complete the book jacket in Lesson 48. See the instructions below to make your book jacket.

☐ Create an introduction to *Kidnapped* on the inside front cover flap by describing the historic setting in which the story takes place. Setting is a very important literary element in historic fiction. *Kidnapped* takes place in Scotland in 1751 following the uniting of England and Scotland into one kingdom. Describe the political situation in Scotland during this time. Include information about the union of England and Scotland, tension between the Jacobites (highlanders) and the Whigs (lowlanders) in Scotland, George II, James Stuart, and Prince Charles Edward. You will find some information in your last reading in KFH but you will need to do some outside research for more information.

A few helpful Web sites:
- en.wikipedia.org/wiki/Jacobitism
- www.shmoop.com/kidnapped/setting.html
- www.sparknotes.com/lit/kidnapped/

☐ Create a biography of Robert Louis Stevenson on the inside back cover flap. Include information on other books he has written. Biographical information can be found in your copy of *Kidnapped* and on the Web.

A helpful Web site:
- www.robert-louis-stevenson.org/index.php

Instructions for creating a book jacket:

(These instructions assume you have a 5" x 7" paperback edition. If your book is a different size, you will need to modify the measurements accordingly.) Cut the construction paper down to 7¾″ by 16½″. Position the paper in landscape orientation and fold in both ends 3 inches. This forms the inside flaps for the front and back covers. From the right-side fold line, measure in 5 inches and make another fold in. Do the same thing from the left side. This will form your front and back covers and leaves a half-inch strip down the middle for the book spine. Turn your paper over—this is the side on which you will glue your work.

Cut out each template on the Book Jacket Template worksheet. You can create your front cover, back cover, inside cover flaps, and the spine right on the templates. When finished, glue the completed templates onto the construction paper in the proper places. Alternatively, you can write directly on the construction paper and not use the templates, or you can glue computer printouts to the construction paper.

When the book jacket is completed (in Lesson 48), cover your copy of *Kidnapped* and tape the inside flaps to the inside covers of the book. If you wish, you can cover the book jacket with contact paper before taping it into your book.

Lesson 47 *Kidnapped* (cont.)

GET READY For this lesson you will need:

- *Kidnapped*

☐ Read *Kidnapped* by Robert Louis Stevenson in two weeks or less. When finished, complete the assignments in the next two lessons.

Lesson 48 *Kidnapped* (cont.)

GET READY For this lesson you will need:

- *Kidnapped*
- Book jacket supplies from Lesson 46

☐ Complete the book jacket for *Kidnapped*. Create a summary of the story for the back cover. Create a front cover with the title and author, and add a picture depicting your favorite scene in *Kidnapped*. The spine should have the title and the author. Glue your completed templates to the folded construction paper and fold the jacket onto the book as you were instructed in Lesson 46.

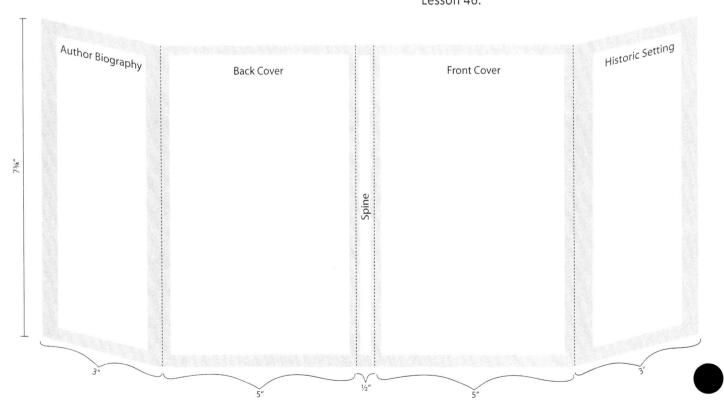

Literary Element: Theme

GET READY For this lesson you will need:

- *Kidnapped*
- Worksheet: Essay Worksheet
- Worksheet: Essay Rubric Checklist

☐ Read the following lesson on theme:

Literary elements are characteristics of works of fiction. Analyzing literary elements can give you a better understanding of a literary work. Some common literary elements are plot, characterization, conflict, point of view, setting, and theme. You have already learned a little bit about setting and its importance in historic fiction. Today you will learn about theme.

The theme is the underlying idea that the author returns to time and time again. It is usually a universal truth, a moral, or a significant underlying statement made about society, human nature, or the human condition. The author may state directly what the theme is (an explicit theme) but more often the theme is inferred or implied (an implicit theme). Most literary works have a theme, and many, such as *Kidnapped*, have several themes. Usually there is one major theme in a story and several minor ones.

Theme is sometimes confused with subject, but they are different and it is important to be able to distinguish between the two. The subject is the topic that is being written about. The theme expresses an opinion or lesson. For example, the subject of *Cinderella* is "a prince falls in love with a poor girl." The theme is "kindness and hard work pay off." Usually the theme of a literary work is expressed through the main character. A good way to determine the theme of a story is to ask yourself what lesson or lessons did the main character learn.

Examples of literary themes include ambition, jealousy, beauty, loneliness, betrayal, love, courage, friendship, loyalty, fear, prejudice, freedom, happiness, and truth. Sometimes a theme can be summed up in just one word, such as "courage." But often the theme is more specific than that. For example "people fear what they do not understand" is a more specific theme than "fear."

Try to determine a specific major theme for the following popular stories. When you have finished, turn the page for possible answers. (No peeking!)

Charlie and the Chocolate Factory by Roald Dahl
Green Eggs and Ham by Dr. Seuss
Hansel and Gretel by Brothers Grimm

☐ Choose one of the themes from *Kidnapped* listed below and write an essay explaining the theme. Begin your essay with the topic sentence "An important theme found in *Kidnapped* by Robert Louis Stevenson is _____." Explain why this is an important theme in the story and include at least three examples (using some direct quotes) from the story. Each example from the story could be a paragraph in your essay. Don't forget to also include introduction and conclusion paragraphs. Use the Essay worksheet and Essay Rubric Checklist to formulate and improve you essay. You can use one of these themes or you can create your own.

Themes:

1. Good conquers evil.

2. Loyalty.

3. The fit will survive.

4. There is good and bad in everyone.

5. True friendship can survive anything.

Possible answers for Lesson 49:

Charlie and the Chocolate Factory - virtue and goodness will be rewarded

Green Eggs and Ham - don't judge things before you try them

Hansel and Gretel - don't talk to strangers

The Rise of Prussia and the Decline of Austria

GET READY For this lesson you will need:

- Map 15, The Seven Years' War (Europe)
- Fine-point black pen or pencil
- Atlas
- KFH
- TSOM (optional)
- Worksheet: Record of War or Conflict

☐ On Map 15, use your atlas to label France, Italy, Germany, England, and Spain. Label water areas. In your atlas find the modern-day names of the countries that occupy the area once known as Prussia.

☐ Read KFH p. 292 "Austria and Prussia."

☐ Read TSOM chapter 49 "The Rise of Prussia."

☐ Write a short biography (a few paragraphs) on **Frederick the Great** in your Men & Women section. Include the improvements he made to Prussia, how he began to build a new German kingdom, and why he was called "Great." Also add a couple of sentences on **Maria Theresa**.

☐ Summarize the War of Austrian Succession by completing a "Record of War or Conflict" worksheet. Place the completed worksheet in the Wars & Conflicts section of your binder.

☐ Add significant dates to your timeline.

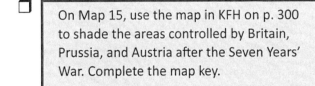

The Seven Years' War and the Fight for North America

GET READY For this lesson you will need:

- KFH
- Map 15, The Seven Years' War (Europe)
- Fine-point black pen or pencil
- Colored pencils

☐ Read KFH pp. 300 - 301 about the Seven Years' War in which European nations battle for control of Europe and colonies.

☐ On Map 15, use the map in KFH on p. 300 to shade the areas controlled by Britain, Prussia, and Austria after the Seven Years' War. Complete the map key.

☐ Add **William Pitt** to your Men & Women section along with a short summary. Save room for more later.

☐ Add the Seven Years' War to your timeline.

The Seven Years' War (cont.)

GET READY For this lesson you will need:

- KFH
- Worksheet: Record of War or Conflict (2)
- Map 16, The Seven Years' War (North America)
- Colored pencils
- Fine-point black pen or pencil
- Atlas

☐ Read KFH pp. 302 - 303 "North America," about the Seven Years' War and the fighting among the French and British colonists in America.

☐ Complete two copies of the "Record of War or Conflict" worksheet for this reading. Create one for the series of battles fought between the French and British colonists and one for Pontiac's Rebellion.

On Map 16, use the map on p. 302 in KFH and your atlas to label:

Canada	Montreal
North America	Boston
Louisiana	Philadelphia
Florida	Quebec
The Great Lakes	St. Pierre
Gulf of Mexico	Miquelon
Atlantic Ocean	

Draw and shade the areas controlled by the British, the French, the Spanish, and Indian territory as indicated in KFH. Complete the map key.

☐ Add significant dates to your timeline.

Lesson 53 The Seven Years' War (cont.)

GET READY For this lesson you will need:

- Worksheet: Storyboard
- Colored pencils
- Fine-point black pen or pencil

☐ Create a storyboard for the Seven Years' War.

Storyboards are used by film makers in the early stages of planning a movie in order to pitch a movie idea in an organized way. A storyboard visually tells and organizes the story, panel by panel, like a comic book. Locate the storyboard worksheets. Pretend you are making a short movie on the Seven Years' War and tell the story of the war, frame by frame on these worksheets. Each rectangle represents one scene. In the top part write a couple of sentences describing the scene. In the larger bottom portion draw a picture of the scene. Number the scenes in the top left corner of each rectangle. Most commonly, storyboards are drawn in pen or pencil. If you don't like to draw you can cut out pictures from magazines or use clip art on a computer to make your storyboards. Keep in mind that your drawings don't have to be fancy! In fact, you can spend just a few minutes drawing each frame using basic shapes, stick figures, maps,

and simple backgrounds. There were many different countries fighting for many different areas during this war. Organize the events, dates of battles, and locations in order to make you storyboard flow smoothly. Make additional copies of the storyboard worksheet if necessary. Place the completed storyboard in the Wars & Conflicts section of your binder.

Some helpful Web sites:

- www.thecanadianencyclopedia.com/articles/seven-years-war
- www.socialstudiesforkids.com/articles/ushistory/frenchandindianwar1.htm

Example of a scene from a Seven Years' War storyboard:

Lesson 54 The Enlightenment

GET READY For this lesson you will need:

- KFH
- Worksheet: The Enlightenment

☐ Read KFH pp. 306 - 307 "The Age of Logic."

☐ In the Men & Women section of your binder add the following along with a short summary:

Voltaire (pronounced vol-TARE)
Denis Diderot (pronounced DEE-dare-oh)
Adam Smith
Immanuel Kant
Thomas Paine (save room to add more later)
Samuel Johnson
Jean-Jacques Rousseau (pronounced roo-SOH, save room to add more later)

☐ Locate the worksheet titled "The Enlightenment." Write advances made in knowledge, justice, science, philosophy, arts, freedom, and liberty during the Enlightenment. Place the completed worksheet in the Summaries section of your binder.

☐ Add significant dates to your timeline.

Lesson 55 *The Island of the Blue Dolphins*

GET READY For this lesson you will need:

- *The Island of the Blue Dolphins* by Scott O'Dell
- Worksheet: Character Comparison Chart

☐ Begin reading *Island of the Blue Dolphins* by Scott O'Dell. Continue with your lessons while you are reading. Start by reading the historic setting introduction found at the end of the book.

☐ While reading, complete the first column on the worksheet titled "Character Comparison Chart." You will be completing this chart after reading *The Sign of the Beaver* in Lesson 87.

Lesson 56 Russia

GET READY For this lesson you will need:

- KFH
- Map 12, 18th Century Russia
- Fine-point black pen or pencil
- Atlas

☐ Read KFH pp. 310 - 311 "Modernizing Russia."

☐ Outline this reading. Place your outline in the Summaries section of your binder.

☐ On Map 12, which you began back in Lesson 34, use the map in KFH to label the Ottoman Empire, Siberia, Mongolia, Moscow, St. Petersburg, Archangel, and Europe. Compare the size of Russia on your map to modern-day Russia in your atlas.

☐ Add **Catherine the Great** to your Men & Women section along with a short summary.

☐ Add significant dates to your timeline.

Lesson 57 Russia (cont.)

GET READY For this lesson you will need:

- Appendix G: *A Journey from St. Petersburg to Moscow*
- Worksheet: Evaluating Sources in History

☐ Read the excerpt from *A Journey from St. Petersburg to Moscow* located in Appendix G. This book was written by Alexander Radishchev, an early Russian intellectual, in 1790. In his book Radishchev reveals the suffering and repression of Russian peasants that he encountered on his travels. While Europe was resolving the issue of peasant serfdom as seen in the Middle Ages, the vast majority of Russian peasants were treated like slaves by the government, producing the agricultural exports that the Russian economy depended on. This created a public relations problem for Russia because repression of peasants conflicted with Western ideas of the Enlightenment. Writers such as Radishchev helped to eventually end serfdom in Russia, but not until well into the nineteenth century.

☐ Complete a copy of the worksheet titled "Evaluating Sources in History" for this excerpt.

☐ Challenge: Write an essay contrasting the life of a peasant to the life of Catherine the Great, landowners, and other royalty in Russia. Include your thoughts on Russian serfdom—Did Russia have a choice? Were there alternatives? How does serfdom conflict with the ideas of the Enlightenment? Begin your essay with a topic sentence about Russian serfdom.

Johnny Tremain

GET READY For this lesson you will need:

- *Johnny Tremain* by Esther Forbes

☐ Begin reading *Johnny Tremain*. Continue with the next lesson while you read but finish by Lesson 60.

Thomas Paine

GET READY For this lesson you will need:

- Appendix H: Excerpts from *Common Sense*
- Worksheet: Evaluating Sources in History

☐ Read the excerpts from *Common Sense* written by Thomas Paine located in Appendix H. This pamphlet, originally published anonymously in 1776, was the first to encourage the American colonists to consider their right to be free of English rule, eventually leading to the American Revolution.

A complete copy of Common Sense can be read online at:
- www.constitution.org/tp/comsense.htm

☐ Complete a copy of the worksheet titled "Evaluating Sources in History" for *Common Sense*. In the summaries portion of the worksheet, explain Paine's major arguments against monarchy and hereditary succession. Also identify the important arguments made for American independence from England.

Persuasive Writing

GET READY For this lesson you will need:

- *Johnny Tremain*
- Worksheet: Brochure Template (optional)

☐ Finish reading *Johnny Tremain*.

☐ Choose one of the two following persuasive writing assignments:

1. As you have read, setting is an important literary element in historic fiction. To describe the historic setting found in *Johnny Tremain*, create a tri-fold travel brochure for pre-revolutionary Boston. Your travel brochure should be written to persuade someone to want to visit Boston in 1773. Include information about the location and geography, recreation, entertainment, the political environment (watch out for those redcoats and don't drink the tea!), climate, food, educational opportunities, how people live, shops, dress, and famous historic figures they might see. You might want to include drawings, maps, or print out images for your brochure. You can use the "Brochure Template" found in the worksheet section, use a design program that has a brochure template option (e.g. Microsoft Publisher, Adobe Illustrator, or Corel), or use purchased brochure paper from a print and copy store or office supply store.

2. Pretend you are a colonist in early America. Write a two-page letter to a friend or family member back in England encouraging (persuading) them to make the move to America. Explain the benefits of living in America but also include warnings of the hardships and current political situation.

The American Revolution

GET READY For this lesson you will need:

- TSOM (optional)
- KFH
- Worksheet: Revolution
- Worksheet: Record of War or Conflict

☐ Read TSOM chapter 51 "The American Revolution."

☐ Read KFH pp. 316 - 317 "The Birth of the U.S.A."

☐ Complete one copy of the "Revolution" worksheet for the American Revolution. Does the American Revolution match one or more of your definitions of a revolution? If so, circle or highlight the definition(s) it matches. Complete the rest of the worksheet. Place the completed worksheet in the Wars & Conflicts section of your binder.

☐ Summarize the American Revolution by completing a "Record of War or Conflict" worksheet. Place the completed worksheet in the Wars & Conflicts section of your binder.

The American Revolution (cont.)

GET READY For this lesson you will need:

- *The American Revolution* by Bruce Bliven, Jr.

☐ From your readings in the last lesson, add the following people to your Men & Women section along with short summaries regarding their role in the American Revolution. (As you read *The American Revolution* add to the descriptions.)

> **William Pitt** (add to your former entry)
> **George Washington**
> **Charles III**
> **Thomas Jefferson**
> **Charles Townshend**
> **Benjamin Franklin**
> **John Adams**
> **John Hancock**
> **Captain Preston**
> **Lord North**
> **Paul Revere**
> **General Gage**
> **Benedict Arnold**
> **Thomas Paine** (add to former entry)

☐ Begin reading *The American Revolution* by Bruce Bliven, Jr. This short book gives an excellent review of the events leading up to the Revolution and the American's fight for freedom. Finish this book within one week, before Lesson 65.

The American Revolution (cont.)

☐ Choose one of the men listed above and write a biography. Place the completed biography in the Men & Women section of your binder.

The American Revolution (cont.)

GET READY For this lesson you will need:

- Appendix I: Accounts of the Boston Massacre
- Worksheet: Evaluating Sources in History (2)

☐ Read accounts of the Boston Massacre from two different sources located in Appendix I.

☐ Complete "Evaluating Sources in History" worksheets for both of these accounts, highlighting the different views of the same event.

The American Revolution (cont.)

GET READY For this lesson you will need:

- Worksheet: Causes of the American Revolution

☐ Locate the worksheet titled "Causes of the American Revolution." Based on the readings and your writings from the last several lessons—KFH, TSOM, *Johnny Tremain*, *Common Sense*, *The American Revolution*, the Revolution worksheet, and the accounts of the Boston Massacre—compile ten events, situations, and/or people that had a hand in causing the American Revolution.

As you have read, the English settlers were initially satisfied to be British and had no intention of forming a separate country when first settling America. Many events changed their minds. Your job here is to identify ten of them. Some examples are the end of the French and Indian War, Mercantilism, the first Continental Congress, pamphlet writers, George Washington, and the Stamp Act. There are many others.

First, list the selections in chronological order, then write a description of each one and its effect or contribution to the American Revolution. Finally, rate each selection with one to four stars according to the importance you feel it played in causing the Revolution. Place your worksheet in the Summaries section of your binder.

Web sites about the causes of the American Revolution:
· www.historycentral.com/Revolt/causes.html
· www.amrevonline.org/museum/exhibition.cgi?page_id=9903
· www.collectionscanada.gc.ca/confederation/023001-3010.52-e.html (the Quebec Act of 1774)
· hoover.archives.gov/exhibits/RevAmerica/3-When/Shot.html (The Shot Heard "Round the World")

☐ Add significant dates to your timeline.

Carry On, Mr. Bowditch (optional)

GET READY   For this lesson you will need:

· *Carry On, Mr. Bowditch* by Jean Lee Latham

☐ Read *Carry on, Mr. Bowditch*. Return to this lesson when you complete the book for an assignment.

You have learned about the literary elements known as setting and theme. Another literary element is characterization. Characterization is the author's method of conveying to the reader a character's personality, attitude, values, and physical attributes. Characterization can be shown through character descriptions such as descriptions of the character's dress and mannerisms. In *Carry on, Mr. Bowditch* one way we get to know each character is through the use of dialogue. Many of the characters have distinct speech patterns and favorite phrases that convey the character's personality and attitude.

For example Nathaniel Bowditch often says "sail by an ash breeze." This was actually a shipping term that referred to the use of oars to move a ship when there was no wind. But to Nathaniel this meant not allowing obstacles to keep him from pursuing his goals. Through this dialogue we learn that Nathaniel is patient, determined, and steadfast. Other sayings common in the book include "stumbling on people's dumbness," "becalmed," "sailing by the book," and "splicing the main brace."

☐ Choose one character in *Carry on, Mr. Bowditch* who has interesting dialogue and write an essay describing the character. Include several quotes made by the character and describe how the character attributes are conveyed through the character's dialogue.

Carry On, Mr. Bowditch - cont. (optional)

GET READY   For this lesson you will need:

● *Carry On, Mr. Bowditch*
● Map 17, The Voyages of Nathaniel Bowditch
● Atlas
● Colored pencils
● Fine-point black pen or pencil

☐ Use your atlas to locate and label the places Nathaniel Bowditch traveled on Map 17, "The Voyages of Nathaniel Bowditch." Then draw each voyages using a different colored pencil and complete the map key.

Voyage #1:   Salem →across the Atlantic → around Africa → Isle of Bourbon (Reunion Island)

Voyage #2:   Salem →across the Atlantic → Lisbon, Portugal →Funchal in the Madeira Islands (off the northwest coast of Africa) →around Africa →across the Indian Ocean →Manila Harbor (the Philippines)

Voyage #3: Salem →across the Atlantic → Cadiz, Spain (a seaport in southwest Spain) →across the Mediterranean Sea →Alicante, Spain (a seaport in southeast Spain)

Voyage #4: Boston → across the Atlantic Ocean → around Africa → across Indian Ocean →Batavia (now known as Jakarta, a seaport of Indonesia on the northwest coast of Java) → Manila Harbor (the Philippines)

Voyage # 5: Salem →across the Atlantic → around Africa → across the Indian Ocean →Sumatra (a western island of Indonesia)

68 "The Way to Wealth"

GET READY For this lesson you will need:

- Appendix J: "The Way to Wealth" by Benjamin Franklin
- Worksheet: Evaluating Sources in History
- Worksheet: "The Way to Wealth" Maxim Meanings

☐ Read Benjamin Franklin's "The Way to Wealth," located in Appendix J.

Benjamin Franklin's ideas on wealth and work helped to create economic policies in America and the idea of the "American Dream." He preached that everyone is created equal, and prosperity was available to all those who worked hard. Believe it or not, this was a novel idea back in the 18th century in the age of "divine right," when people achieved wealth primarily through inheritance or through their position in society. Benjamin Franklin published his ideas about economics in *Poor Richard's Almanac*. "The Way to Wealth" was published in the last edition in 1758.

☐ Complete an "Evaluating Sources In History" worksheet for this reading.

☐ Locate the worksheet titled "The Way to Wealth" Maxim Meanings. For each maxim (or proverb) listed, write an interpretation of its meaning in relation to wealth, business, and economics.

69 The Bill of Rights

GET READY For this lesson you will need:

- Appendix K: The Bill of Rights

Have you ever read the Constitution of the United States or the constitution of the country you live in? A constitution is the supreme law of a country. If you haven't, now would be a good time to do so. If you do not have a copy in your home or school, you can find a copy on the Internet or at your library.

Every now and then amendments are added to a constitution. The United States Bill of Rights was the first amendment made to the U.S. Constitution. It was made in 1791, three years after the initial Constitution. Its purpose was to limit the powers of the government and protect the powers of the people.

☐ Read the United States Bill of Rights located in Appendix K.

If you live in another country, locate a copy of the comparable document from your country. In Canada this document is called the Canadian Charter of Rights and Freedoms and can be read at:

- laws.justice.gc.ca/en/Charter/index.html.

☐ Imagine your country without the rights that this document ensures. Choose one of the rights and write an essay describing how life would be different if your countrymen did not have this right. Create a topic sentence stating the importance of the right you chose. Think of three situations or circumstances where not having this right would create a difficulty, a hardship, a dangerous situation, a violation of basic individual rights, etc. Each situation could be a paragraph in your essay. Don't forget to include introduction and conclusion paragraphs. Have your essay checked for grammar and spelling and place a completed copy in the summaries section of your binder.

70 The End of Slavery?

GET READY For this lesson you will need:

- KFH
- Map 8, Africa and the Slave Trade, 16th to 19th Centuries
- Atlas
- Fine-point black pen or pencil

☐ Read KFH pp. 308 - 309 "Africa."

☐ On Map 8, which you began in Lesson 23, draw and identify new African states as indicated on p. 308 of KFH. Look in your Atlas to see if these are the modern-day names of African states. Also label Morocco, Yemen, and Egypt.

☐ Read KFH pp. 322 - 323 "The End of Slavery."

☐ Add the following people to your Men & Women section along with short summaries:

Nat Turner (read picture caption)
William Wilberforce
Thomas Clarkson
Jean-Jacques Rousseau (add to your former entry)

Lesson 71 The End of Slavery? (cont.)

GET READY   For this lesson you will need:

• Worksheet: A Timeline of Slavery

☐ On the worksheet titled "A Timeline of Slavery." Create a vertical timeline of slavery on this worksheet. Record significant dates for slavery beginning with the 1600s and ending with 1888 and the abolishment of slavery in Brazil. Record the date, the event, and the place the event occurred. Some dates will be ranges such as "French colony of Santo Domingo 1791-1793 - Slave revolt." Give each event a reference number that refers to a location on the world map. Refer back to Lessons 23 - 25 for earlier events.

☐ Add any dates not previously recorded on your main timeline.

☐ Challenge: Research modern-day slavery and add dates to your vertical timeline. Record how and where slavery is practiced today.

Lesson 72 The French Revolution

GET READY   For this lesson you will need:

• KFH
• TSOM (optional)

☐ Read KFH pp. 318 - 319 "The French Revolution."

☐ Create a three-level outline on this reading.

☐ Read TSOM chapter 52 "The French Revolution."

☐ Add significant dates to your timeline.

Lesson 73 The French Revolution (cont.)

GET READY   For this lesson you will need:

• Worksheet: Revolution
• Worksheet: Record of War or Conflict
• KFH
• TSOM (optional)

☐ Complete one copy of a Revolution worksheet for the French Revolution. Does the French Revolution match one or more of your definitions of a revolution? If so, circle or highlight the definition(s) it matches. Complete the rest of the worksheet. Place the completed worksheet in the Wars & Conflicts section of your binder.

☐ Summarize the French Revolution by completing a Record of War or Conflict worksheet. Place the completed worksheet in the Wars & Conflicts section of your binder.

☐ Add the following to your Men & Women section along with short summaries. You will find information in KFH and in your reading from TSOM.

Marie Antoinette
Maximillion Robespierre
Louis XVI
Napoleon Bonaparte
Montesquieu (pronounced *mon-tess-cue*)
Rousseau (add to your former entry)
Diderot (add to your former entry)

Lesson 74 Make the Connection

GET READY   For this lesson you will need:

• Appendix L: Excerpts from the Age of Reason and the Enlightenment

In this lesson you will examine the connections between the Scientific Revolution and the Enlightenment to the revolutions around the world, specifically the American Revolution and the French Revolution.

It may be hard to imagine that there could be a connection between advances in physics, astronomy, and philosophy to political revolution, but that was the case in the 18th century. The philosophical and scientific writers during the period of the Enlightenment and the Scientific Revolution greatly influenced the revolutions that took place in America and France.

☐ Read excerpts from the writings of Locke, Paine, Rousseau, and Montesquieu located in Appendix L. Review the work you did on the Scientific Revolution and the Enlightenment in Lessons 11 - 15 and 54.

☐ Choose one central idea of the Scientific Revolution and one from the Enlightenment that relate to democratic thought, authority, liberty, and government. Write the ideas on the top of a page in your Summaries section. (The ideas can be several sentences or may be paragraphs.) Describe how each writing in Appendix L reflects the ideas of the Scientific Revolution and the Enlightenment that you chose. Use quotes from the excerpts in your description. Then, in a separate paragraph, describe how the ideas affected the American and French revolutions. You may need to review the work you completed on these revolutions in Lessons 61 to 65 covering the American Revolution and Lessons 72 and 73 covering the French Revolution.

The Napoleonic Wars

GET READY For this lesson you will need:

- KFH
- Worksheet: Record of War or Conflict
- Map 18, The French Empire Under Napoleon (1812)
- Atlas
- Fine-point black pen or pencil
- Colored pencils

☐ Read KFH pp. 320 - 321 "The Napoleonic Wars."

☐ Complete a Record of War or Conflict worksheet for the Napoleonic Wars. Place the completed worksheet in the Wars & Conflicts section of your binder.

☐ On Map 18, use your atlas to label the following:

Italy	Spain
Switzerland	Holland
Denmark	Sardinia
Baltic Sea	Black Sea
Corsica	Portugal
France	Great Britain
Russia	Africa
Mediterranean Sea	Paris

Shade the area of French Empire (within the dotted lines) and complete the map key.

☐ Record significant dates on your timeline.

Napoleon - Hero or Zero?

GET READY For this lesson you will need:

- TSOM (optional)
- Appendix M: "The Two Grenadiers"
- Encyclopedias, Internet, and/or library access
- Worksheet: Evaluating Sources in History

☐ Research secondary and primary sources on the life of Napoleon. Use at least two print sources in your research.

Recommended video:
PBS miniseries *Napoleon* by director David Grubin (2000)

Recommended web sites:
· www.pbs.org/empires/napoleon (PBS biographical information)
· europeanhistory.about.com/od/ bonapartenapoleon/a/bionapoleon.htm (biography information)
· www.napoleon-series.org/research/government/c_ code.html (information about Napoleon's code)

☐ Read TSOM chapter 53 "Napoleon."

☐ Read "The Two Grenadiers" located in Appendix M.

☐ Write a commentary on Napoleon as if you are writing for a newspaper at the time of Napoleon. Decide whether you want to present Napoleon as a tyrant or a hero. To assist you in writing your commentary, it might helpful to complete "Evaluating Sources in History" worksheets for each source you read or watch about Napoleon. To prepare for writing a commentary, read commentaries and opinion articles in your local newspapers. Notice the different styles used. In a commentary, don't be afraid to state a strong opinion. But you will need to support your opinion of Napoleon with specific examples from his life. Don't forget to include introductory and concluding paragraphs in your commentary.

Lesson 77 The Congress of Vienna

GET READY For this lesson you will need:

- TSOM (optional)

In 1815, in an effort to undo the overwhelming domination of the French by Napoleon, five European countries (Prussia, Russia, Austria, Great Britain, and France) convened in Vienna, Austria. Their task was to redistribute European boundaries and come up with a peaceful end to the Napoleonic Era. The changes they made to Europe lasted 65 years.

☐ Read TSOM chapter 54, which gives a rather lively and cynical summary of the goings-on at the Congress and some of the key players - Talleyrand of France, Metternich of Austria, Castleregh of Britain, and Alexander I of Russia (and his baroness Krüdener).

☐ Read TSOM chapter 55, which summarizes the results of the Congress.

☐ Optional: View the map on this Web site:

- https://www2.bc.edu/~heineman/maps/1815label. html

Compare the map of Europe after the Congress of Vienna to Map 18. Notice the changes in Europe—the reestablishment of Switzerland and Poland, Italy still divided into several kingdoms, the decrease in the size of the French Empire, etc.

☐ Summarize the Congress of Vienna in your Summaries section. Describe its purpose, decisions that were made, important participants, and how the Congress reestablished a balance of power and a time of peace (albeit a short one).

A couple of informative web sites:

- www.the-map-as-history.com/demos/tome01/index. php (a good site for information and maps)
- encyclopedia.kids.net.au/page/co/Congress_of_ Vienna

Lesson 78 Latin America's Fight for Freedom

GET READY For this lesson you will need:

- KFH
- Map 19, Latin America 1808 - 1830
- Atlas
- Fine-point black pen or pencil
- Colored pencils

Latin America was strongly influenced by the American Revolution, the French Revolution, and feelings of nationalism. In 1808, Central and South America fought for independence from Spanish and Portuguese rule.

☐ Read KFH p. 326 "Revolt in Latin America."

☐ Summarize the revolt in Latin America in the Wars & Conflicts section of your binder.

☐ Add **Simón Bolivar** and **José de San Martin** to the Men & Women section of your binder along with short summaries.

☐ On Map 19, use KFH p. 326 to draw the boundaries of each Latin American country and label the following (add dates of liberation to each country):

Argentina	Mexico	Peru
Uruguay	Pacific Ocean	Dutch Guiana
Venezuela	Bolivia	Ecuador
Atlantic Ocean	French Guiana	Brazil
Chile	Columbia	British Guiana
Paraguay	Gulf of Mexico	
Central American Federation		

> Find Latin America in your atlas. Write the modern-day names of these areas in parentheses if different. Shade each area a different color.

☐ Add significant dates to your timeline.

Lesson 79
Nationalism and Revolution in Europe

GET READY For this lesson you will need:

- TSOM (optional)
- KFH
- Presentation software (optional)

☐ Read TSOM chapter 56 "National Independence."

☐ Read KFH pp. 346 - 347 "Europe: Year of Revolution."

☐ Create a presentation on nationalism (also called liberal nationalism) and the Revolutions of 1848 using presentation software, such as PowerPoint, Keynote, or Corel Presentations. (If you do not have access to presentation software then give a traditional oral report.)

In your presentation define *nationalism* and discuss how it grew out of the French Revolution, the Napoleonic Era, and the Congress in Vienna. Describe how feelings of nationalism contributed to revolutions across Europe. Describe the revolutions that took place in different parts of Europe—focusing on France, Austria, Prussia (Germany), and Italy. Finally describe the results of the revolutions. Use charts, maps, pictures, and other effects in your presentation.

A couple of informative Web sites:

· www.preceden.com/timelines/46464-european-nationalism-timeline (timeline of revolutions)
· ap_history_online.tripod.com/apeh10h.htm

☐ Give your presentation or oral report to your family and friends! Have a picture of taken of you giving your presentation and put it in your Summaries section along with any notes or outlines you created.

Lesson 80
Australia and New Zealand

GET READY For this lesson you will need:

- KFH
- Map 20, Oceania Discovered
- Colored pencils
- Fine-point black pen or pencil

☐ Read KFH pp. 312 - 313 "Exploration in Oceania."

☐ Create a three-level outline on this reading titled "Exploration of Oceania." Place your completed outline in the Summaries section of your binder.

☐
> On Map 20, draw the route of Captain James Cook as presented in KFH p. 312. Label Australia, New Zealand, Tasmania, New South Wales, Gulf of Carpentaria, Pacific Ocean, and Indian Ocean. Complete the map key.

☐ Read KFH pp. 348 - 349 "New Zealand."

☐ Write a two- to four-paragraph description of the Maori in the Men & Women section of your binder. Include information about their customs, their religion, the Treaty of Waitangi, and conflicts with the British.

☐ Add the following to your Men & Women section along with short summaries:

Abel Tasman
William Dampier
Captain James Cook
The Aborigines

☐ Add significant dates to your timeline.

Lesson 81
Growth of the United States

GET READY For this lesson you will need:

- KFH
- Worksheet:Record of War or Conflict (4)

In 1803, Thomas Jefferson was president when the United States purchased territory that contained all of present-day Louisiana, Arkansas, Missouri,

Iowa, Oklahoma, Kansas, Nebraska, Minnesota south of the Mississippi River, much of North Dakota, nearly all of South Dakota, northeastern New Mexico, northern Texas, portions of Montana, Wyoming, and Colorado east of the Continental Divide. Called "The Louisiana Purchase," this acquisition nearly doubled the size of the United States. The U.S. purchased this territory from Napoleon at the cost of about 3¢ per acre in order to take the control of the seaport in New Orleans from the French.

- ☐ Read KFH pp. 328 - 329 "Westward Migration."

- ☐ Read KFH p. 342 "Texas and Mexico."

- ☐ Summarize the following conflicts in your Wars & Conflicts section by completing a "Record of War or Conflict" worksheet for each one:

    The War of 1812

    The Alamo

    The Mexican-American War

    The Trail of Tears (for maps and more information visit: www.pbs.org/indiancountry/history/trail.html)

☐ On Map 21, label Canada, Gulf of Mexico, Atlantic Ocean, Pacific Ocean, Missouri River, Lake Superior, Lake Michigan, and Lake Huron.

Shade the territory of the original thirteen colonies, area ceded by Great Britain in 1783, the Louisiana Purchase, the Texas Annexation, the Oregon Territory, the Spanish Cession, the Mexican Cession, and other acquisitions different colors.

- ☐ Research and briefly summarize each of these United States acquisitions by creating a vertical timeline on a page in your Summaries section. Begin with the Treaty of Paris in 1783, in which Great Britain ceded the area of the thirteen colonies and end with the Treaty of Guadalupe-Hidalgo in 1848 in which Mexico ceded California and other Western states. Include when the acquisition was made, from whom, and under what circumstances.

Helpful Web sites:
- en.wikipedia.org/wiki/United_States_territorial_acquisitions
- www.u-s-history.com/pages/h1049.html
- geography.about.com/od/politicalgeography/a/usboundary.htm

Lesson 82 — Growth of the United States (cont.)

GET READY For this lesson you will need:

- KFH
- Map 21, United States Territories
- Atlas
- Colored pencils
- Fine-point black pen or pencil
- Encyclopedias, Internet, and/or library access

☐ From your readings in the last lesson, add the following to your Men & Women section along with brief summaries:

Meriwether Lewis
William Clark
Andrew Jackson
Sam Houston
Santa Anna
Davy Crockett

Lesson 83 — Growth of the United States (cont.)

☐ Choose one person from the last lesson and write a biography. Use at least two print sources in your research. Don't forget to include a bibliography. Place the completed biography in the Men & Women section of your binder.

Lesson 84 Lewis and Clark

GET READY For this lesson you will need:

- Map 21, United States Territories
- Atlas
- Colored pencils
- Fine-point black pen or pencil
- *The Captain's Dog* by Roland Smith

☐ On Map 21, draw the route of Lewis and Clark—began in St. Louis, traveled along the Missouri River, and traveled across Oregon to the west coast. Complete the map key.

☐ Read *The Captain's Dog*. When you finish proceed to the next lesson for an assignment.

☐ As you read, add **Sacajawea** to the Men & Women section of your binder.

☐ For more information on Lewis and Clark and the Corps of Discovery, visit: www.pbs.org/lewisandclark

or watch the Ken Burns documentary: *Lewis and Clark: The Journey of the Corps of Discovery.*

Print resources are listed in Appendix N.

Lesson 85 Literary Element: Point of View

☐ Read the following lesson on point of view:

On July 20th, 1969 the crew of Apollo 11 *landed. For the first time a person, Neil Armstrong, set foot on the moon. Neil Armstrong was frightened and excited, millions of people watched in awe from their television sets, and the NASA crew held their breath listening to Neil Armstrong's now famous words, "One small step for a man, one giant leap for mankind."*

There are many points of view from which the story of *Apollo 11* could be told—Neil Armstrong's, the NASA crew's, or a child's as he is watching on his new black and white TV set. A fictional story could even be written from the moon's point of view, describing how it felt to have a person visit for the first time. Or it could be told by a narrator, who can see everything and know everyone's thoughts and feelings. The story of *Apollo 11* would be different when told from each of these points of view.

Point of view is the angle from which a story is told. The tone, feeling, and facts of a story will change depending on the point of view from which it is told. There are several different types of point of view:

First-Person

In first-person, one of the characters from the story is telling the story and can reveal only personal thoughts and feelings. He (or she) reveals what he sees and is told by other characters. This character can't see into the mind of the other characters to tell us their thoughts or feelings. When the storyteller is using words like "I" or "we" then the story is most likely written in first-person.

Third-Person

In third-person, someone outside the story is telling it. This person is called a narrator and they are not a part of the story.

There are different types of third-person point of view:

1. Third-Person Objective: The narrator is an outsider (not part of the story) who can report only what he or she sees and hears. The narrator can tell us what is happening, but can't tell us the thoughts or feelings of the characters. This type of point of view has been called the "fly on the wall" perspective because a fly is not a part of what is going on and can see all that is happening but can't know what people are thinking.

2. Omniscient Limited (also called Third-Person Limited): The narrator is an outsider who sees into the mind of only one of the characters.

3. Omniscient: The narrator is an all-knowing outsider who can enter the minds of all (or at least more than one) of the characters.

☐ In the Summaries section of your binder summarize first-person point of view and the different types of third-person point of view.

☐ Discuss with your parent or teacher the difference between first-person and omniscient limited.

☐ Take the following event and write a short story five times, from each of the points of view listed above—first-person, third-person objective, omniscient limited, and omniscient. Tell the story twice from first-person (once from the Chickasaw's point of view and once from the bear's). (A few sentences for each point of view is all that you need to write.)

A Chickasaw boy, crouching behind a boulder, is sweating and short-of-breath as he carefully watches a large black bear greedily eat wild blueberries.

☐ Discuss with your parent or teacher the point of view from which *The Captain's Dog* is told. Is it first-person or third-person? Who is telling the story? How would the story have been different if told from another point of view? Do you think you would you have liked the story as well?

☐ List the books you have read in this course in the Summaries section of your binder. After each title, write the point of view found in the story.

Lesson 86 — The Sign of the Beaver

GET READY For this lesson you will need:

• *The Sign of the Beaver* by Elizabeth George Speare

☐ In two to three days read *The Sign of the Beaver*. When finished, go on to the next lesson for an assignment.

Lesson 87 — Compare and Contrast

GET READY For this lesson you will need:

• *The Sign of the Beaver*
• *Island of the Blue Dolphins*
• Worksheet: Character Comparison Chart
• Worksheet: Character Comparison Venn Diagram

☐ You have read two stories about abandonment and survival—*The Sign of the Beaver* and *Island of the Blue Dolphins*. You may have also read *Robinson Crusoe* in the past. In each of these stories the main character finds himself or herself stranded and struggles to survive. On the worksheet titled "Character Comparison Chart," you have already completed the column for Karana. Now complete the worksheet by recording how Matt and Crusoe (if read) dealt with each situation on the chart.

When you have completed the chart, complete the "Character Comparison Venn Diagram" worksheet. Record the situations that are unique to Karana in her circle and those unique to Matt in his circle. Where the circles intersect write the items they have in common. (If you are including Crusoe in your comparison, then create your own Venn diagram using three circles.)

☐ Using the Venn diagram and the chart, write a four-paragraph essay comparing and contrasting Karana and Matt (and Crusoe if you wish). Start by writing an introductory paragraph where you introduce the characters and the stories. State in your opening paragraph how the characters are alike and how they are different. This will be your topic sentence. In the next paragraph describe in detail how the characters and their situations are alike. In the third paragraph describe in detail how they and their situations are different. In the final paragraph write a conclusion that summarizes your assessment and comparison of these characters.

☐ Have your parent or teacher edit your essay for content and grammar. Write or type a final copy and file it in the Summaries section of your binder.

Revolution Around the World

GET READY For this lesson you will need:

- Worksheet: Revolution Around the World
- Colored pencils

☐ Locate the worksheet titled "Revolution Around the World." In each box on the map, write one or two major events that occurred during this time in that region of the world. Also include names of significant inventors, artists, scientists, leaders, and writers. Use information from the readings, writing assignments, and timeline entries you have completed in the second part of this course. Draw a line from each box to its appropriate place on the map. Color the map and place it in your Summaries section.

Timeline Analysis

GET READY For this lesson you will need:

- Worksheet: Timeline Analysis

You have spent the last year recording early modern history dates from different regions of the world on your timeline. At times you have been jumping all over your timeline, going back and forth from 1600 to 1850. An enormous amount occurred during these 250 years. Now that you have completed your study of early modern history, it is time to analyze your timeline chronologically. You might be amazed by what you find.

☐ To do this analysis you will use the Timeline Analysis worksheet. Start at the beginning of early modern history on your timeline and look at what was happening on different continents of the world during the first time span on your chart (1600 - 1625). Also look in the different sections of your binder and on the worksheets you completed for events. Write all of these events in their proper places on the table. Continue this for each time period. You do not need to recopy your entire timeline! That is not the purpose of this exercise. The purpose is for you to notice the similarities, connections, and great differences between events that were occurring in the world at the same time. Pick and choose those events that you feel best reflect each time span. There will be some blanks on the table.

Below is an example of what your table might look like for the time span of 1600 - 1625. Notice that while Japan was isolated and Australia had not yet been explored, there were many connections occurring elsewhere in the world. The European religious wars and discrimination caused the Puritans to settle colonies in America. New colonies in America contributed to the need for slaves and slave plantations in the West Indies. The slave trade increased the development of Africa and its connection to Europe.

☐ When you have completed the table, choose four to five time spans where either a surprising difference, a powerful connection, or an incredible coincidence occurred. Summarize these events in paragraph form and place in the Summaries section of your binder.

	North America	South America	Africa	Europe	Asia	Oceania
1600 - 1625	Puritans founded Jamestown	Slaves traded and brought to the West Indies	Developed many different states, trading with Europe	Protestants and Catholics begin Thirty Years' War	Japan seals itself off from the rest of the world	

Attribution of Sources

When conducting research for the writing assignments in this course, you will be reading books and passages written by other people. If you want to use the writings of others in your summaries, essays, and your research paper, you will need to *paraphrase* the work or *quote* the author and then attribute (give credit for) the work to the author. Proper attribution of sources is very important and helps you to avoid plagiarism. *Plagiarism* is presenting someone else's work as your own or not properly attributing an idea to the author. Plagiarism can be a serious offense. At many colleges and high schools, students receive a failing grade if they plagiarize. Also, you should be aware that professors have sophisticated software and resources to assist them in detecting plagiarism.

PARAPHRASING AND QUOTING

Paraphrasing is restating a passage and conveying its meaning with different words. To paraphrase correctly, you need to restate the original author's ideas in your own words. Simply changing a few words in a sentence is not paraphrasing. The best way to paraphrase is to begin by thoroughly reading the passage you want to paraphrase. Then close the book and rewrite the idea without looking at the original work. Be sure to cite all of the authors and their works from which you borrowed ideas in the bibliography at the end of your report (see bibliography examples on the next page).

A *quote* is the exact words of the author placed in quotation marks. When using a quote, state the words *exactly* as the author did. Most of the time it is more appropriate to paraphrase an author than to directly quote him or her. But occasionally you will want to use a quote. You might want to use a quote when the words of the author are particularly powerful, when you are quoting a line in literature, or when using the words of a famous person. For example:

When Rousseau said, "Man is born free, and everywhere he is in chains," he implied that people are hindered by the limitations of their government.

Punctuation in quotations can be tricky. Refer to your grammar book or a writing handbook, like those published by the MLA, to learn proper punctuation when using direct quotes.

BIBLIOGRAPHY

A bibliography is a list of the books, articles, Internet sites, and audiovisuals from which you gathered information when preparing your report. When do you need to cite a source in a bibliography? Basically, you need to cite any source from which you borrow an idea, use direct quotes, or write a paraphrase in your report. You do not need to cite a source when the knowledge is common knowledge. For example, information about Napoleon that indicates he was a successful general of the French army who crowned himself emperor in 1804 does not need to be attributed because this information is common history knowledge.

When writing a bibliography, you should . . .
• Put the sources in alphabetical order by the author's last name or by the first word of the title if there is no author (not counting "a," "an," or "the").
• Indent the second line of an entry if you need to use more than one line.
• Skip a line after each entry.
• Underline the title of a book or magazine (or use italics if typing).

- List the authors in the order they are listed on the title page when there is more than one author.
- List the title of an article from a newspaper of encyclopedia before the name of the newspaper or encyclopedia. Put titles of articles in quotation marks.

BIBLIOGRAPHY EXAMPLES*

BOOK:

Author's last name, first name. *Title of book*. Place of publication: Publisher, copyright year.

Example:

Yates, Elizabeth. *Amos Fortune, Free man*. New York: Puffin Books, 1950.

ENCYCLOPEDIA ARTICLE WITHOUT AN AUTHOR:

"Title of article." *Name of encyclopedia*. Edition number. Copyright year.

Example:

"Civil War Heroes." *World Book Encyclopedia*. 10th ed. 1999.

MAGAZINE OR NEWSPAPER ARTICLE:

Article author's last name, first name. "Title or headline of article." *Name of magazine or newspaper*. Date of magazine or newspaper, section and page.

Example:

Jacobs, Ernie. "War Casualties Rise." *New York Times*. May 10th, 2007, A1.

INTERNET ADDRESS:

Author's last name, first name. "Title of item." Date of document or download. http://address If there is no author cited, then begin with the title.

Example:

"BookRags Short Guide on Kidnapped." January 29, 2007. www.bookrags.com/shortguide-kidnapped

FILM:

Title of film. Director. Distributor, year of release.

Example:

It's a Wonderful Life. Dir. Frank Capra. RKO, 1946.

* According to the MLA. Gibaldi, Joseph. *MLA Handbook for Writers of Research Papers*. 6th ed. New York: The Modern Language Association of America, 2003.

How to Write a Biography

A biography is a story about a person's life. When you write about yourself, it is called an autobiography. A biography can be a paragraph in length or long enough to make a book. For this course, your biographies should be one to five pages in length (less if typed). Obviously, in this course, your biographies will be about people who lived a long time ago. When writing a biography on a living person, you would be wise to interview the person if possible. When writing about a person from the past, you will have to depend on primary sources, historians, and other biographers. Primary sources are especially important. A primary source is any record from the actual time period in which the person lived. A primary source could be an autobiography written by the person you are studying, documents from the time period, or writings from witnesses to the events.

The first step to writing a biography is to research the person's life. You can use encyclopedias, your local library, and/or information on the internet. Take notes while you are researching. Locate information about the person's birth, death, childhood, good and bad deeds, obstacles he/she overcame, the effect he/she had on history, time period and environment, family and friends, and other important or interesting aspects of his/her life.

Next, decide how you want to write the biography and make an outline from your notes. A biography can be written in linear fashion by starting at the person's birth and continuing with events in chronological order, ending with his/her death. You may choose to write about one important aspect or event in the person's life or focus on a few different themes. The choice is yours. Organize your notes by completing an outline. Write each major point in a biography as a main topic. Each main topic should be a paragraph in your biography. Then organize the details under each main topic.

The last step to writing a biography is to create a true story. Biographies are much more interesting when told as a story with characters, plot, conflict, and emotion that brings the person to life. Use your outline to guide your writing. Finally, give your biography a title and show off your work!

For more information on writing an interesting biography see The Biography Maker at
http://fno.org/bio/biomaker.htm.

Guidelines for Evaluating Sources in History

When evaluating sources in history you will need to consider the type of document, the intended audience, the purpose of the work, the reliability/validity, and whether or not it is a primary or secondary source.

Accounts in history can be either primary sources or secondary sources. A **primary source** is a document from the time period, an artifact (object, picture, photograph, etc.) made by a person from the time period, or an account by a witness to the event. Speeches, letters, eyewitness testimonies, photographs, and government documents are considered primary sources. **Secondary sources** are interpretations and analysis of history produced by someone who was not directly involved in the event. Writings by historians and drawings found in your history encyclopedias are secondary sources.

Consider the **type** of work you are analyzing. Is it a document that was intended to be public or private? Examples of types of works are: newspaper articles, books, magazine articles, government documents and records, speeches, advertisements, maps, pamphlets, posters, photographs, drawings, letters, journals, diary entries, oral histories or stories, biographies, and autobiographies.

Consider the **intended audience** of the work. Examples of intended audiences are the general public, a specific group of people like the citizens of the United States or of New York City, one individual as in the case of a private letter, or the writer himself as in the case of a diary entry.

Consider the **purpose** of the work. Is the work intended to inform or persuade? Was the work written to instruct or to inspire? The intended audience and the type of work will give you clues as to the purpose of the work.

When you **summarize** the work, rewrite it in your own words. Include all of the main points without giving your opinion or assessing the work. If the work is an artifact (picture, drawing, statue, map, etc.) place an image of the work, sketch the artifact, or describe it.

Reliability or **validity** indicates the overall truthfulness of a source. All of the above information (type, audience, and purpose) will help you to determine if a source is reliable or valid. The other factors that determine reliability/validity are time and place. The closer the author is to the time and place in which the event happened, usually the more valid the source is. Obviously the purpose (to inform or persuade) will also help. The level of reliability and validity also determine how dependable a source is. To know the dependability of the work you will need to know information about the author or the organization for which they work. What biases does the author have that may affect the reliability of the work? What is the author's point of view—neutral or interested in taking a side? How educated about the event is the author? What are his credentials? What organizations does he belong to or what affiliations does he have? Can you verify the information? Did the author have firsthand knowledge of the event? All of these questions will help you to determine the level of reliability/validity. While you might think that primary sources have a higher reliability and validity than secondary sources, you can evaluate primary sources for factual content and consider author's intention. (Was he or she over emphasizing or distorting information to make a point and get a certain reaction from the intended audience?) State whether you feel the source is valid and reliable or not. Also state whether the reliability/validity is high, medium, or low and explain why you have come to that conclusion.

The Crime of Galileo, 1633

INDICTMENT OF GALILEO:

Whereas you, Galileo, son of the late Vincenzio Galilei, of Florence, aged seventy years, were denounced in 1615, to this Holy Office, for holding as true a false doctrine taught by many, namely, that the sun is immovable in the center of the world, and that the earth moves, and also with a diurnal motion; also, for having pupils whom you instructed in the same opinions; also, for maintaining a correspondence on the same with some German mathematicians; also for publishing certain letters on the sun-spots, in which you developed the same doctrine as true; also, for answering the objections which were continually produced from the Holy Scriptures, by glozing the said Scriptures according to your own meaning; and whereas thereupon was produced the copy of a writing, in form of a letter professedly written by you to a person formerly your pupil, in which, following the hypothesis of Copernicus, you include several propositions contrary to the true sense and authority of the Holy Scriptures; therefore (this Holy Tribunal being desirous of providing against the disorder and mischief which were thence proceeding and increasing to the detriment of the Holy Faith) by the desire of his Holiness and the Most Emminent Lords, Cardinals of this supreme and universal Inquisition, the two propositions of the stability of the sun, and the motion of the earth, were qualified by the Theological Qualifiers as follows:

1. The proposition that the sun is in the center of the world and immovable from its place is absurd, philosophically false, and formally heretical; because it is expressly contrary to Holy Scriptures.

2. The proposition that the earth is not the center of the world, nor immovable, but that it moves, and also with a diurnal action, is also absurd, philosophically false, and, theologically considered, at least erroneous in faith.

Therefore . . . , invoking the most holy name of our Lord Jesus Christ and of His Most Glorious Mother Mary, We pronounce this Our final sentence: We pronounce, judge, and declare, that you, the said Galileo . . . have rendered yourself vehemently suspected by this Holy Office of heresy, that is, of having believed and held the doctrine (which is false and contrary to the Holy and Divine Scriptures) that the sun is the center of the world, and that it does not move from east to west, and that the earth does move, and is not the center of the world; also, that an opinion can be held and supported as probable, after it has been declared and finally decreed contrary to the Holy Scripture, and, consequently, that you have incurred all the censures and penalties enjoined and promulgated in the sacred canons and other general and particular constituents against delinquents of this description. From which it is Our pleasure that you be absolved, provided that with a sincere heart and unfeigned faith, in Our presence, you abjure, curse, and detest, the said error and heresies, and every other error and heresy contrary to the Catholic and Apostolic Church of Rome.

And to the end that this thy grave error and transgression remain not entirely unpunished, and that thou mayst be more cautious in the future, and an example to others to abstain from and avoid similar offences,

We order that by a public edict the book of DIALOGUES OF GALILEO GALILEI be prohibited, and We condemn thee to the prison of this Holy Office during Our will and pleasure; and as a salutary penance We enjoin on thee that for the space of three years thou shalt recite once a week the Seven Penitential Psalms, reserving to Ourselves the faculty of moderating, changing, or taking from, all other or part of the above-mentioned pains and penalties.

And thus We say, pronounce, declare, order, condemn, and reserve in this and in any other better way and form which by right We can and ought.

Ita pronunciamus nos Cardinalis infrascripti.

F. Cardinalis de Asculo.	B. Cardinalis Gypsius.
G. Cardinalis Bentivolius	F. Cardinalis Verospius.
D. Cardinalis de Cremona.	M. Cardinalis Ginettus.
A. Cardinalis S. Honuphri.	

GALILEO'S ABJURATION:

I, Galileo Galilei, son of the late Vincenzio Galilei of Florence, aged 70 years, tried personally by this court, and kneeling before You, the most Eminent and Reverend Lord Cardinals, Inquisitors-General throughout the Christian Republic against heretical depravity, having before my eyes the Most Holy Gospels, and laying on them my own hands; I swear that I have always believed, I believe now, and with God's help I will in future believe all which the Holy Catholic and Apostolic Church doth hold, preach, and teach.

But since I, after having been admonished by this Holy Office entirely to abandon the false opinion that the Sun was the centre of the universe and immoveable, and that the Earth was not the centre of the same and that it moved, and that I was neither to hold, defend, nor teach in any manner whatever, either orally or in writing, the said false doctrine; and after having received a notification that the said doctrine is contrary to Holy Writ, I did write and cause to be printed a book in which I treat of the said already condemned doctrine, and bring forward arguments of much efficacy in its favour, without arriving at any solution: I have been judged vehemently suspected of heresy, that is, of having held and believed that the Sun is the centre of the universe and immoveable, and that the Earth is not the centre of the same, and that it does move.

Nevertheless, wishing to remove from the minds of your Eminences and all faithful Christians this vehement suspicion reasonably conceived against me, I abjure with sincere heart and unfeigned faith, I curse and detest the said errors and heresies, and generally all and every error and sect contrary to the Holy Catholic Church. And I swear that for the future I will neither say nor assert in speaking or writing such things as may bring upon me similar suspicion; and if I know any heretic, or one suspected of heresy, I will denounce him to this Holy Office, or to the Inquisitor and Ordinary of the place in which I may be.

I also swear and promise to adopt and observe entirely all the penances which have been or may be by this Holy Office imposed on me. And if I contravene any of these said promises, protests, or oaths, (which God forbid!) I submit myself to all the pains and penalties which by the Sacred Canons and other Decrees general and particular are against such offenders imposed and promulgated. So help me God and the Holy Gospels, which I touch with my own hands.

I Galileo Galilei aforesaid have abjured, sworn, and promised, and hold myself bound as above; and in token of the truth, with my own hand have subscribed the present schedule of my abjuration, and have recited it word by word. In Rome, at the Convent della Minerva, this 22nd day of June, 1633.

I, GALILEO GALILEI, have abjured as above, with my own hand.

How to Write an Essay

An assignment to write an essay can be daunting and even scary, especially if you have never written an essay. But essay writing does not have to be difficult if you have a model to assist in directing and organizing your ideas. Here you will be given just such a model. As you become better at writing essays, you can veer away from this model and be more creative with the organization of your essays.

An essay is a short literary composition on a single subject that often expresses an opinion. Essays differ from reports and summaries. Reports are generally several pages long and don't usually express an opinion. The biographies you will be writing in this course are a form of a short report. Summaries are quick summations of information that you take from another source and paraphrase in your own words. Summaries don't express an opinion, and style and organization aren't as important.

The model you will be using to write essays requires you to *select a topic*, develop a *topic sentence*, organize your materials in *pre-writing*, produce a *draft copy*, *edit* your draft, and *publish* your work by producing a final copy.

Step 1: Selecting a Topic

In this course, your topic is often selected for you in the lesson. If it isn't, or if you are given a choice of topics, then select one you are interested in and about which you think you could find enough information to write several paragraphs. Begin to research the topic. In this course, your research will consist of the course readings, literature readings, and outside research in encyclopedias, at the library, and on the Internet. Sometime during your research you will develop a topic sentence (see Step 2). After developing the topic sentence, gear your research toward finding supporting evidence. Supporting evidence consists of specific examples that support your topic sentence. Evidence can be quotes from a book or person, excerpts from documents, opinions of experts, and other supporting information.

Step 2: Developing a Topic Sentence

This step may occur before or during your research in Step 1. A topic sentence summarizes what your essay is about in a succinct and specific way. It is related to but different than the topic. First of all, the topic sentence is a sentence, while a topic is usually a word or phrase. Secondly, the topic sentence announces the topic and makes an assertion about it. The topic sentence often portrays a side to an issue or an opinion about the topic. Think of the topic sentence as "the topic with attitude." For example, "Beekeeping" is a topic, and "Beekeeping is a rewarding hobby" is a topic sentence. The topic sentence also narrows the topic and makes it manageable for an essay. You could write a book about beekeeping, but the rewards of beekeeping as a hobby could be confined to an essay. Make sure that your topic sentence conveys only one idea about the topic, not two or three. The topic sentence is the first sentence or the last sentence in the introductory paragraph of your essay.

Step 3: Pre-writing

Organize into an outline the information you obtained doing research. Write your topic sentence as the title of the outline. Select approximately three main ideas (or points) that support your topic sentence. These three main ideas will become Roman numerals I, II, and III in your outline. Under each main idea, write supportive evidence as A, B, and C. Try to have at least three items of supportive evidence; that way you will have enough information to make each main idea a paragraph in your essay. After you complete the outline, you are ready to format your essay into paragraphs in the next step.

Example of an essay outline:

Beekeeping is a rewarding hobby.

    I. Benefits of hive construction
       A. Making hives
       B. Educational
       C. Companionship
    II. Benefits of pollination
       A. Fruit trees produce more fruit
       B. Gardens produce more vegetables
       C. Helping the community
    III. Benefits of honey
       A. Adventures of farming honey
       B. Delicious
       C. Nutritious

Step 4: Drafting

To assist you in this process, locate the "Essay Worksheet." Now, using the outline you created in Step 3, write the topic sentence in the first box and each main idea (Roman numerals in your outline) in the three boxes under the topic sentence. The introduction is created from your topic sentence and your main ideas. In this paragraph you will "introduce" your essay topic. Begin or end this paragraph with your topic sentence and state your main ideas.

The body of your essay will consist of three paragraphs if you created three main ideas. State the main idea as the first sentence in the paragraph. Use the supportive evidence (A, B, and C in your outline) to create the rest of the paragraph. Do the same for each main idea. Try to make each paragraph approximately five sentences long. To make your essay flow, begin each sentence in the body of your essay with transitional words. Here is a list of commonly used transitional words:

First, second, third	Consequently
To begun with, in addition, finally	However
Furthermore, also	Even though
Therefore	Another
Thus	On the other hand
As a result of	Nevertheless

The conclusion paragraph is a summary of what you have already expressed in the body paragraphs. Do not state any new ideas in the conclusion. Sum up the essay's main points but be careful that you do not restate them exactly. You can insert your assessment of the topic or express an opinion in the conclusion paragraph.

Now, rewrite or type what you have written on the worksheet onto a new sheet of paper, creating a draft copy of your five-paragraph essay.

Step 5: Editing

Read over your draft copy and check it for spelling, punctuation, and grammar. Also make sure your essay is organized and flows from one paragraph to another. Consider your choice of words, making sure you have not repeated a word too many times and that you have used powerful adjectives. Consider using a thesaurus to find word alternatives. The Essay Rubric Checklist found in this guide will assist you with editing your work.

After you correct any mistakes you find, give your essay and the Essay Rubric Checklist to a parent, teacher, or advisor. Have him or her read your draft and ask for advice on how you can improve it.

Step 6: Revising and Publishing

You're almost done! In this step you simply rewrite or type your essay, correcting any mistakes made on the draft and taking into account any advice you were given during editing. Carefully check your revised copy for any mistakes as you did in Step 4. When it looks good, place a final copy in your binder and voilà—you are finished and your essay is "published"!

APPENDIX F

First Hand Account of the Slave Trade

The following excerpt comes from Alexander Falconbridge's book written in 1788, *An Account of the Slave Trade on the Coast of Africa*. Employed as a surgeon aboard various slave ships, Falconbridge had firsthand knowledge of many aspects of the slave trade.

From the time of the arrival of the ships to their departure, which is usually near three months, scarce a day passes without some negroes being purchased, and carried on board; sometimes in small, and sometimes in larger numbers. The whole number taken on board, depends, in a great measure, on circumstances. In a voyage I once made, our stock of merchandize was exhausted in the purchase of about 380 negroes, which was expected to have procured 500. . .

Previous to my being in this employ I entertained a belief, as many others have done, that the kings and principal men bred Negroes for sale as we do cattle. . . . When the Negroes, whom the black traders have to dispose of [or sell], are shown to the European purchasers, they first examine them relative to their age. They then minutely inspect their persons and inquire into the state of their health; if they are afflicted with any disease or are deformed or have bad eyes or teeth; if they are lame or weak in the joints or distorted in the back or of a slender make or narrow in the chest; in short, if they have been ill or are afflicted in any manner so as to render them incapable of much labor. If any of the foregoing defects are discovered in them they are rejected. But if approved of, they are generally taken on board the ship the same evening. The purchaser has liberty to return on the following morning, but not afterwards, such as upon re-examination are found exceptionable.

The traders frequently beat those Negroes which are objected to by the captains and use them with great severity. It matters not whether they are refused on account of age, illness, deformity or for any other reason. At New Calabar, in particular, the traders have frequently been known to put them to death. Instances have happened at that place, when Negroes have been objected to, that the traders have dropped their canoes under the stern of the vessel and instantly beheaded them in sight of the captain. . . .

Nor do these unhappy beings, after they become the property of the Europeans (from whom, as a more civilized people, more humanity might naturally be expected), find their situation in the least amended. Their treatment is no less rigorous. The men Negroes, on being brought aboard the ship, are immediately fastened together, two and two, by handcuffs on their wrists and by irons riveted on their legs. They are then sent down between the decks and placed in an apartment partitioned off for that purpose. The women also are placed in a separate apartment between decks, but without being ironed. An adjoining room on the same deck is appointed for the boys. Thus they are all placed in different apartments.

But at the same time, however, they are frequently stowed so close, as to admit of no other position than lying on their sides. Nor will the height between decks, unless directly under the grating, permit the indulgence of an erect posture; especially where there are platforms, which is generally the case. These platforms are a kind of shelf, about eight or nine feet in breadth, extending from the side of the ship toward the centre. They are placed nearly midway between the decks, at the distance of two or three feet from each deck, Upon these the Negroes are stowed in the same manner as they are on the deck underneath.

In each of the apartments are placed three or four large buckets, of a conical form, nearly two feet in diameter at the bottom and only one foot at the top and in depth of about twenty-eight inches, to which, when necessary, the Negroes have recourse. It often happens that those who are placed at a distance from the buckets, in endeavoring to get to them, rumble over their companions, in consequence of their being shackled. These accidents, although unavoidable, are productive of continual quarrels in which some of them are always bruised. In this distressed situation, unable to proceed and prevented from getting to the tubs, they desist from the attempt; and as the necessities of nature are not to be resisted, ease themselves as they lie. This becomes a fresh source of boils and disturbances and tends to render the condition of the poor captive wretches still more uncomfortable. The nuisance arising from these circumstances is not infrequently increased by the tubs being much too small for the purpose intended and their being usually emptied but once every day. The rule for doing so, however, varies in different ships according to the attention paid to the health and convenience of the slaves by the captain....

The diet of the Negroes while on board, consists chiefly of horse beans boiled to the consistency of a pulp; of boiled yams and rice and sometimes a small quantity of beef or pork. The latter are frequently taken from the provisions laid in for the sailors. They sometimes make use of a sauce composed of palm-oil mixed with flour, water and pepper, which the sailors call slabber-sauce. Yams are the favorite food of the Eboe or Bight Negroes, and rice or corn of those from the Gold or Windward Coast; each preferring the produce of their native soil....

Upon the Negroes refusing to take sustenance, I have seen coals of fire, glowing hot, put on a shovel and placed so near their lips as to scorch and burn them. And this has been accompanied with threats of forcing them to swallow the coals if they any longer persisted in refusing to eat. These means have generally had the desired effect. I have also been credibly informed that a certain captain in the slave-trade, poured melted lead on such of his Negroes as obstinately refused their food....

The hardships and inconveniences suffered by the Negroes during the passage are scarcely to be enumerated or conceived. They are far more violently affected by seasickness than Europeans. It frequently terminates in death, especially among the women. But the exclusion of fresh air is among the most intolerable. For the purpose of admitting this needful refreshment, most of the ships in the slave trade are provided, between the decks, with five or six air-ports on each side of the ship, of about five inches in length and four in breadth. In addition, some ships, but not one in twenty, have what they denominate wind-sails. But whenever the sea is rough and the rain heavy it becomes necessary to shut these and every other conveyance by which the air is admitted. The fresh air being thus excluded, the Negroes' rooms soon grow intolerable hot. The confined air, rendered noxious by the effluvia exhaled from their bodies and being repeatedly breathed, soon produces fevers and fluxes which generally carries off great numbers of them.

During the voyages I made, I was frequently witness to the fatal effects of this exclusion of fresh air. I will give one instance, as it serves to convey some idea, though a very faint one, of their terrible sufferings.... Some wet and blowing weather having occasioned the port-holes to be shut and the grating to be covered, fluxes and fevers among the Negroes ensued. While they were in this situation, I frequently went down among them till at length their room became so extremely hot as to be only bearable for a very short time. But the excessive heat was not the only thing that rendered their

situation intolerable. The deck, that is the floor of their rooms, was so covered with the blood and mucus which had proceeded from them in consequence of the flux, that it resembled a slaughter-house. It is not in the power of the human imagination to picture a situation more dreadful or disgusting. Numbers of the slaves having fainted, they were carried upon deck where several of them died and the rest with great difficulty were restored. It had nearly proved fatal to me also. The climate was too warm to admit the wearing of any clothing but a shirt and that I had pulled off before I went down.... In a quarter of an hour I was so overcome with the heat, stench and foul air that I nearly fainted, and it was only with assistance I could get back on deck. The consequence was that I soon after fell sick of the same disorder from which I did not recover for several months...

This devastation, great as it was, some years ago was greatly exceeded by a Leverpool ship . . . This ship, though a much smaller ship than in which I have just mentioned, took on board at Bonny at least six hundred Negroes . . . By purchasing so great a number, the slaves were so crowded that they were obliged to lie one upon another. This caused such a mortality among them that without meeting with unusually bad weather or having a longer voyage than common, nearly one half of them died before the ship arrived in the West Indies....

The place allotted for the sick Negroes is under the half deck, where they lie on the bare planks. By this means those who are emaciated frequently have their skin and even their flesh entirely rubbed off, by the motion of the ship, from the prominent parts of the shoulders, elbows and hips so as to render the bones quite bare. ...

As very few of the Negroes can so far brook the loss of their liberty and the hardships they endure, they are ever on the watch to take advantage of the least negligence in their oppressors. Insurrections are frequently the consequence; which are seldom expressed without much bloodshed. Sometimes these are successful and the whole ship's company is cut off. They are likewise always ready to seize every opportunity for committing some acts of desperation to free themselves from their miserable state and notwithstanding the restraints which are laid, they often succeed....

The mode of selling them by scramble having fallen under my observation the oftenest, I shall be more particular in describing it. Being some years ago, at one of the islands in the West Indies, I was witness to a sale by scramble, where about 250 Negroes were sold. Upon this occasion all the Negroes scrambled for bear an equal price; which is agreed upon between the captains and the purchasers before the sale begins. On a day appointed, the Negroes were landed and placed together in a large yard belonging to the merchants to whom the ship was consigned. As soon as the hour agreed on arrived, the doors of the yard were suddenly thrown open and in rushed a considerable number of purchasers, with all the ferocity of brutes. Some instantly seized such of the Negroes as they could conveniently lay hold of with their hands. Others being prepared with several handkerchiefs tied together, encircled as many as they were able. While others, by means of a rope, effected the same purpose. It is scarcely possible to describe the confusion of which this mode of selling is productive....

APPENDIX G

Excerpts from:
A Journey from St. Petersburg to Moscow

I suppose it is all the same to you whether I traveled in winter or in summer. Maybe both in winter and in summer. It is not unusual for travelers to set out in sleighs and to return in carriages. In summer, the corduroy road tortured my body; I climbed out of the carriage and went on foot. While I had been lying back in the carriage, my thoughts had turned to the immeasurable vastness of the world. By spiritually leaving the earth I thought I might more easily bear the jolting of the carriage. But spiritual exercises do not always distract us from our physical selves; and so, to save my body, I got out and walked. A few steps from the road I saw a peasant ploughing a field. The weather was hot. I looked at my watch. It was twenty minutes before one. I had set out on Saturday. It was now Sunday. The ploughing peasant, of course, belonged to a landed proprietor, who would not let him pay a commutation tax [obrok]. The peasant was ploughing very carefully. The field, of course, was not part of his master's land. He turned the plough with astonishing ease.

"God help you," I said, walking up to the ploughman, who, without stopping, was finishing the furrow he had started. "God help you," I repeated.

"Thank you, sir," the ploughman said to me, shaking the earth off the ploughshare and transferring it to a new furrow.

"You must be a Dissenter, since you plough on a Sunday."

"No, sir, I make the true sign of the cross," he said, showing me the three fingers together. "And God is merciful and does not bid us starve to death, so long as we have strength and a family."

"Have you no time to work during the week, then, and can you not have any rest on Sundays, in the hottest part of the day, at that?"

"In a week, sir, there are six days, and we go six times a week to work on the master's fields; in the evening, if the weather is good, we haul to the master's house the hay that is left in the woods; and on holidays the women and girls go walking in the woods, looking for mushrooms and berries. God grant," he continued, making the sign of the cross, "that it rains this evening. If you have peasants of your own, sir, they are praying to God for the same thing."

"My friend, I have no peasants, and so nobody curses me. Do you have a large family?"

"Three sons and three daughters. The eldest is nine years old."

"But how do you manage to get food enough, if you have only the holidays free?"

"Not only the holidays: the nights are ours, too. If a fellow isn't lazy, he won't starve to death. You see, one horse is resting; and when this one gets tired, I'll take the other; so the work gets done."

"Do you work the same way for your master? "

"No, Sir, it would be a sin to work the same way. On his fields there are a hundred hands for one mouth, while I have two for seven mouths: you can figure it out for yourself. No matter how hard you work for the master, no one will thank you for it. The master will not pay our head tax; but, though he doesn't pay it, he doesn't demand one sheep, one hen, or any linen or butter the less. The peasants are much better off where the landlord lets them pay a commutation tax without the interference of the steward. It is true that sometimes even good masters take more than three rubles a man; but even that's better than having to work on the master's fields. Nowadays it's getting to be the custom to let villages to tenants, as they call it. But we call it putting our heads in a noose. A landless tenant skins us peasants alive; even the best ones don't leave us any time for ourselves. In the winter he won't let us do any carting of goods and won't let us go into town to work; all our work has to be for him, because he pays our head tax. It is an invention of the Devil to turn your peasants over to work for a stranger. You can make a complaint against a bad steward, but to whom can you complain against a bad tenant?"

"My friend, you are mistaken; the laws forbid them to torture people."

"Torture? That's true; but all the same, sir, you would not want to be in my hide." Meanwhile the ploughman hitched up the other horse to the plough and bade me goodbye as he began a new furrow.

The words of this peasant awakened in me a multitude of thoughts. I thought especially of the inequality of treatment within the peasant class. I compared the crown peasants with the manorial peasants. They both live in villages; but the former pay a fixed sum, while the latter must be prepared to pay whatever their master demands. The former are judged by their equals; the latter are dead to the law, except, perhaps, in criminal cases. A member of society becomes known to the government protecting him, only when he breaks the social bonds, when he becomes a criminal! This thought made my blood boil.

Tremble, cruelhearted landlord! on the brow of each of your peasants I see your condemnation written.

. . . [I saw in a peasant's home that] the upper half of the four walls, and the whole ceiling, were covered with soot. The floor was full of cracks and covered with dirt at least two inches thick; the oven without a smoke-stack, but their best protection against the cold; and smoke filling the hut every morning, winter and summer; window holes over which were stretched bladders which admitted a dim light at noon time; two or three pots (happy the hut if one of them each day contains some watery cabbage soup!). Here one justly looks for the source of the country's wealth, power, and might. But here are also seen the weakness, inadequacy, and abuse of the laws: their harsh side, so to speak. Here may be seen the greed of the gentry, our rapaciousness and tyranny; and the helplessness of the poor.

Excerpts from Common Sense by Thomas Paine

Philadelphia, February 14, 1776

Of Monarchy and Hereditary Succession

MANKIND being originally equals in the order of creation, the equality could only be destroyed by some subsequent circumstance; the distinctions of rich, and poor, may in a great measure be accounted for, and that without having recourse to the harsh ill sounding names of oppression and avarice. Oppression is often the consequence, but seldom or never the means of riches; and though avarice will preserve a man from being necessitously poor, it generally makes him too timorous to be wealthy.

But there is another and greater distinction for which no truly natural or religious reason can be assigned, and that is, the distinction of men into KINGS and SUBJECTS. Male and female are the distinctions of nature, good and bad the distinctions of heaven; but how a race of men came into the world so exalted above the rest, and distinguished like some new species, is worth enquiring into, and whether they are the means of happiness or of misery to mankind. . .

To the evil of monarchy we have added that of hereditary succession; and as the first is a degradation and lessening of ourselves, so the second, claimed as a matter of right, is an insult and an imposition on posterity. For all men being originally equals, no one by birth could have a right to set up his own family in perpetual preference to all others for ever, and though himself might deserve some decent degree of honors of his contemporaries, yet his descendants might be far too unworthy to inherit them. One of the strongest natural proofs of the folly of hereditary right in kings, is, that nature disapproves it, otherwise, she would not so frequently turn it into ridicule by giving mankind an ass for a lion.

Secondly, as no man at first could possess any other public honors than were bestowed upon him, so the givers of those honors could have no power to give away the right of posterity, and though they might say "We choose you for our head," they could not, without manifest injustice to their children, say "that your children and your children's children shall reign over ours for ever." Because such an unwise, unjust, unnatural compact might (perhaps) in the next succession put them under the government of a rogue or a fool. Most wise men, in their private sentiments, have ever treated hereditary right with contempt; yet it is one of those evils, which when once established is not easily removed; many submit from fear, others from superstition, and the more powerful part shares with the king the plunder of the rest.

This is supposing the present race of kings in the world to have had an honorable origin; whereas it is more than probable, that could we take off the dark covering of antiquity, and trace them to their first rise, that we should find the first of them nothing better than the principal ruffian of some restless gang, whose savage manners or pre-eminence in subtility obtained him the title of chief among plunderers; and who by increasing in power, and extending his depredations, over-awed the quiet and defenceless to purchase their safety by frequent contributions. Yet his electors could have no idea of giving hereditary right to his descendants, because such a perpetual exclusion of themselves was incompatible with the free and unrestrained principles they professed to live by.

Wherefore, hereditary succession in the early ages of monarchy could not take place as a matter of claim, but as something casual or complimental; but as few or no records were extant in those days, and traditionary history stuffed with fables, it was very easy, after the lapse of a few generations, to trump up some superstitious tale, conveniently timed, Mahomet like, to cram hereditary right down the throats of the vulgar. Perhaps the disorders which threatened, or seemed to threaten, on the decease of a leader and the choice of a new one (for elections among ruffians could not be very orderly) induced many at first to favor hereditary pretensions; by which means it happened, as it hath happened since, that what at first was submitted to as a convenience, was afterwards claimed as a right.

England, since the conquest, hath known some few good monarchs, but groaned beneath a much larger number of bad ones; yet no man in his senses can say that their claim under William the Conqueror is a very honorable one. A French bastard landing with an armed banditti, and establishing himself king of England against the consent of the natives, is in plain terms a very paltry rascally original.—It certainly hath no divinity in it. However, it is needless to spend much time in exposing the folly of hereditary right, if there are any so weak as to believe it, let them promiscuously worship the ass and lion, and welcome. I shall neither copy their humility, nor disturb their devotion.

Yet I should be glad to ask how they suppose kings came at first? The question admits but of three answers, viz. either by lot, by election, or by usurpation. If the first king was taken by lot, it establishes a precedent for the next, which excludes hereditary succession. Saul was by lot, yet the succession was not hereditary, neither does it appear from that transaction there was any intention it ever should. If the first king of any country was by election, that likewise establishes a precedent for the next; for to say, that the right of all future generations is taken away, by the act of the first electors, in their choice not only of a king, but of a family of kings for ever, hath no parrallel in or out of scripture but the doctrine of original sin, which supposes the free will of all men lost in Adam; and from such comparison, and it will admit of no other, hereditary succession can derive no glory. For as in Adam all sinned, and as in the first electors all men obeyed; as in the one all mankind were subjected to Satan, and in the other to Sovereignty; as our innocence was lost in the first, and our authority in the last; and as both disable us from reassuming some former state and privilege, it unanswerably follows that original sin and hereditary succession are parallels. Dishonorable rank! Inglorious connexion! Yet the most subtile sophist cannot produce a juster simile.

As to usurpation, no man will be so hardy as to defend it; and that William the Conqueror was an usurper is a fact not to be contradicted. The plain truth is, that the antiquity of English monarchy will not bear looking into.

But it is not so much the absurdity as the evil of hereditary succession which concerns mankind. Did it ensure a race of good and wise men it would have the seal of divine authority, but as it opens a door to the foolish, the wicked, and the improper, it hath in it the nature of oppression. Men who look upon themselves born to reign, and others to obey, soon grow insolent; selected from the rest of mankind their minds are early poisoned by importance; and the world they act in differs so materially from the world at large, that they have but little opportunity of knowing its true interests, and when they succeed to the government are frequently the most ignorant and unfit of any throughout the dominions.

Another evil which attends hereditary succession is, that the throne is subject to be possessed by a minor at any age; all which time the regency, acting under the cover of a king, have every opportunity and inducement to betray their trust. The same national misfortune happens, when a king worn out with age and infirmity, enters the last stage of human weakness. In both these cases the public becomes a prey to every miscreant, who can tamper successfully with the follies either of age or infancy.

The most plausible plea, which hath ever been offered in favour of hereditary succession, is, that it preserves a nation from civil wars; and were this true, it would be weighty; whereas, it is the most barefaced falsity ever imposed upon mankind. The whole history of England disowns the fact. Thirty kings and two minors have reigned in that distracted kingdom since the conquest, in which time there have been (including the Revolution) no less than eight civil wars and nineteen rebellions. Wherefore instead of making for peace, it makes against it, and destroys the very foundation it seems to stand on.

Thoughts on the Present State of American Affairs

IN the following pages I offer nothing more than simple facts, plain arguments, and common sense: and have no other preliminaries to settle with the reader, than that he will divest himself of prejudice and prepossession, and suffer his reason and his feelings to determine for themselves that he will put on, or rather that he will not put off, the true character of a man, and generously enlarge his views beyond the present day.

Volumes have been written on the subject of the struggle between England and America. Men of all ranks have embarked in the controversy, from different motives, and with various designs; but all have been ineffectual, and the period of debate is closed. Arms as the last resource decide the contest; the appeal was the choice of the King, and the Continent has accepted the challenge...

I have heard it asserted by some, that as America has flourished under her former connection with Great Britain, the same connection is necessary towards her future happiness, and will always have the same effect. Nothing can be more fallacious than this kind of argument. We may as well assert that because a child has thrived upon milk, that it is never to have meat, or that the first twenty years of our lives is to become a precedent for the next twenty. But even this is admitting more than is true; for I answer roundly that America would have flourished as much, and probably much more, had no European power taken any notice of her. The commerce by which she hath enriched herself are the necessaries of life, and will always have a market while eating is the custom of Europe...

But Britain is the parent country, say some. Then the more shame upon her conduct. Even brutes do not devour their young, nor savages make war upon their families. Wherefore, the assertion, if true, turns to her reproach; but it happens not to be true, or only partly so, and the phrase PARENT OR MOTHER COUNTRY hath been jesuitically adopted by the King and his parasites, with a low papistical design of gaining an unfair bias on the credulous weakness of our minds. Europe, and not England, is the parent country of America. This new World hath been the asylum for the persecuted lovers of civil and religious liberty from EVERY PART of Europe. Hither have they fled, not from the tender embraces of the mother, but from the cruelty of the monster; and it is so far true of England, that the same tyranny which drove the first emigrants from home, pursues their descendants still.

But, admitting that we were all of English descent, what does it amount to? Nothing. Britain, being now an open enemy, extinguishes every other name and title: and to say that reconciliation is our duty, is truly farcical. The first king of England, of the present line (William the Conqueror) was a Frenchman, and half the peers of England are descendants from the same country; wherefore, by the same method of reasoning, England ought to be governed by France.

Much hath been said of the united strength of Britain and the Colonies, that in conjunction they might bid defiance to the world. But this is mere presumption; the fate of war is uncertain, neither do the expressions mean anything; for this continent would never suffer itself to be drained of inhabitants, to support the British arms in either Asia, Africa, or Europe.

Besides, what have we to do with setting the world at defiance? Our plan is commerce, and that, well attended to, will secure us the peace and friendship of all Europe; because it is the interest of all Europe to have America a free port. Her trade will always be a protection, and her barrenness of gold and silver secure her from invaders.

I challenge the warmest advocate for reconciliation to show a single advantage that this continent can reap by being connected with Great Britain. I repeat the challenge; not a single advantage is derived. Our corn will fetch its price in any market in Europe, and our imported goods must be paid for buy them where we will.

But the injuries and disadvantages which we sustain by that connection, are without number; and our duty to mankind at large, as well as to ourselves, instruct us to renounce the alliance: because, any submission to, or dependence on, Great Britain, tends directly to involve this Continent in European wars and quarrels, and set us at variance with nations who would otherwise seek our friendship, and against whom we have neither anger nor complaint. As Europe is our market for trade, we ought to form no partial connection with any part of it. It is the true interest of America to steer clear of European contentions, which she never can do, while, by her dependence on Britain, she is made the makeweight in the scale of British politics...

Though I would carefully avoid giving unnecessary offence, yet I am inclined to believe, that all those who espouse the doctrine of reconciliation, may be included within the following descriptions. Interested men, who are not to be trusted, weak men who CANNOT see, prejudiced men who will not see, and a certain set of moderate men who think better of the European world than it deserves; and this last class, by an ill-judged deliberation, will be the cause of more calamities to this Continent than all the other three.

It is the good fortune of many to live distant from the scene of present sorrow; the evil is not sufficiently brought to their doors to make them feel the precariousness with which all American property is possessed. But let our imaginations transport us a few moments to Boston; that seat of wretchedness will teach us wisdom, and instruct us for ever to renounce a power in whom we can have no trust. The inhabitants of that unfortunate city who but a few months ago were in ease and affluence, have now no other alternative than to stay and starve, or turn out to beg. Endangered by the fire of their friends if they continue within the city and plundered by the soldiery if they leave it, in their present situation they are prisoners without the hope of redemption, and in a general attack for their relief they would be exposed to the fury of both armies.

Men of passive tempers look somewhat lightly over the offences of Great Britain, and, still hoping for the best, are apt to call out, "Come, come, we shall be friends again for all this." But examine the passions and feelings of mankind: bring the doctrine of reconciliation to the touchstone of nature, and then tell me whether you can hereafter love, honour, and faithfully serve the power that hath carried fire and sword into your land? If you cannot do all these, then are you only deceiving yourselves, and by your delay bringing ruin upon posterity. Your future connection with Britain, whom you can neither love nor honour, will be forced and unnatural, and being formed only on the plan of present convenience, will in a little time fall into a relapse more wretched than the first. But if you say, you can still pass the violations over, then I ask, hath your house been burnt? Hath your property been destroyed before your face? Are your wife and children destitute of a bed to lie on, or bread to live on? Have you lost a parent or a child by their hands, and yourself the ruined and wretched survivor? If you have not, then are you not a judge of those who have. But if you have, and can still shake hands with the murderers, then are you unworthy the name of husband, father, friend or lover, and whatever may be your rank or title in life, you have the heart of a coward, and the spirit of a sycophant...

As to government matters, it is not in the power of Britain to do this continent justice: The business of it will soon be too weighty, and intricate, to be managed with any tolerable degree of convenience, by a power, so distant from us, and so very ignorant of us; for if they cannot conquer us, they cannot govern us. To be always running three or four thousand miles with a tale or a petition, waiting four or five months for an answer, which when obtained requires five or six more to explain it in, will in a few years be looked upon as folly and childishness — There was a time when it was proper, and there is a proper time for it to cease.

Small islands not capable of protecting themselves, are the proper objects for kingdoms to take under their care; but there is something very absurd, in supposing a continent to be perpetually governed by an island. In no instance hath nature made the satellite larger than its primary planet, and as England and America, with respect to each other, reverses the common order of nature, it is evident they belong to different systems: England to Europe, America to itself...

But the king you will say has a negative in England; the people there can make no laws without his consent. In point of right and good order, there is something very ridiculous, that a youth of twenty-one (which hath often happened) shall say to several millions of people, older and wiser than himself, I forbid this or that act of yours to be law. But in this place I decline this sort of reply, though I will never cease to expose the absurdity of it, and only answer, that England being the King's residence, and America not so, make quite another case. The king's negative here is ten times more dangerous and fatal than it can be in England, for there he will scarcely refuse his consent to a bill for putting England into as strong a state of defence as possible, and in America he would never suffer such a bill to be passed.

America is only a secondary object in the system of British politics, England consults the good of this country, no farther than it answers her own purpose. Wherefore, her own interest leads her to suppress the growth of ours in every case which doth not promote her advantage, or in the least interferes with it. A pretty state we should soon be in under such a second-hand government, considering what has happened! Men do not change from enemies to friends by the alteration of a name: And in order to shew that reconciliation now is a dangerous doctrine, I affirm, that it would be policy in the king at this time, to repeal the acts for the sake of reinstating himself in the government of the provinces; in order that HE MAY ACCOMPLISH BY CRAFT AND SUBTILITY, IN THE LONG RUN,

WHAT HE CANNOT DO BY FORCE AND VIOLENCE IN THE SHORT ONE. Reconciliation and ruin are nearly related...

That as even the best terms, which we can expect to obtain, can amount to no more than a temporary expedient, or a kind of government by guardianship, which can last no longer than till the colonies come of age, so the general face and state of things, in the interim, will be unsettled and unpromising. Emigrants of property will not choose to come to a country whose form of government hangs but by a thread, and who is every day tottering on the brink of commotion and disturbance; and numbers of the present inhabitants would lay hold of the interval, to dispose of their effects, and quit the continent.

But the most powerful of all arguments, is, that nothing but independence, i. e. a continental form of government, can keep the peace of the continent and preserve it inviolate from civil wars. I dread the event of a reconciliation with Britain now, as it is more than probable, that it will followed by a revolt somewhere or other, the consequences of which may be far more fatal than all the malice of Britain...

Ye that tell us of harmony and reconciliation, can ye restore to us the time that is past? Can ye give to prostitution its former innocence? Neither can ye reconcile Britain and America. The last cord now is broken, the people of England are presenting addresses against us. There are injuries which nature cannot forgive; she would cease to be nature if she did. As well can the lover forgive the ravisher of his mistress, as the continent forgive the murders of Britain. The Almighty hath implanted in us these unextinguishable feelings for good and wise purposes. They are the guardians of his image in our hearts. They distinguish us from the herd of common animals. The social compact would dissolve, and justice be extirpated from the earth, or have only a casual existence were we callous to the touches of affection. The robber, and the murderer, would often escape unpunished, did not the injuries which our tempers sustain, provoke us into justice.

O ye that love mankind! Ye that dare oppose, not only the tyranny, but the tyrant, stand forth! Every spot of the old world is overrun with oppression. Freedom hath been hunted round the globe. Asia, and Africa, have long expelled her. — Europe regards her like a stranger, and England hath given her warning to depart. O! receive the fugitive, and prepare in time an asylum for mankind.

The Boston Massacre

Boston Massacre from an American point of view (anonymous source):

. . . We shall next attend to the conduct of the troops, and to some circumstances relative to them. Governor Bernard without consulting the Council, having given up the State House to the troops at their landing, they took possession of the chambers, where the representatives of the province and the courts of law held their meetings; and (except the council-chamber) of all other parts of that house; in which they continued a considerable time, to the great annoyance of those courts while they sat, and of the merchants and gentlemen of the town, who had always made the lower floor of it their exchange. They [the merchants] had a right so to do, as the property of it was in the town; but they were deprived of that right by mere power. The said Governor soon after, by every stratagem and by every method but a forcibly entry, endeavored to get possession of the manufactory-house, to make a barrack of it for the troops; and for that purpose caused it to be besieged by the troops, and the people in it to be used very cruelly;

The General Court, at the first session after the arrival of the troops, viewed it in this light, and applied to Governor Bernard to cause such a nuisance to be removed; but to no purpose.

The challenging the inhabitants by sentinels posted in all parts of the town before the lodgings of officers, which (for about six months, while it lasted), occasioned many quarrels and uneasiness.

Capt. Wilson, of the 59th, exciting the negroes of the town to take away their masters' lives and property, and repair to the army for protection, which was fully proved against him. The attack of a party of soldiers on some of the magistrates of the town-the repeated rescues of soldiers from peace officers-the firing of a loaded musket in a public street, to the endangering a great number of peaceable inhabitants-the frequent wounding of persons by their bayonets and cutlasses, and the numerous instances of bad behavior in the soldiery, made us early sensible that the troops were not sent here for any benefit to the town or province, and that we had no good to expect from such conservators of the peace.

It was not expected, however, that such an outrage and massacre, as happened here on the evening of the fifth instant, would have been perpetrated. There were then killed and wounded, by a discharge of musketry, eleven of his Majesty's subjects, viz.:

APPENDIX I

* Mr. Samuel Gray, killed on the spot by a ball entering his head.

* Crispus Attucks, a mulatto, killed on the spot, two balls entering his breast.

* Mr. James Caldwell, killed on the spot, by two balls entering his back.

* Mr. Samuel Maverick, a youth of seventeen years of age, mortally wounded; he died the next morning.

* Mr. Patrick Carr mortally wounded; he died the 14th instant.

* Christopher Monk and John Clark, youths about seventeen years of age, dangerously wounded. It is apprehended they will die.

* Mr. Edward Payne, merchant, standing at his door; wounded.

* Messrs. John Green, Robert Patterson, and David Parker; all dangerously wounded.

The actors in this dreadful tragedy were a party of soldiers commanded by Capt. Preston of the 29th regiment. This party, including the Captain, consisted of eight, who are all committed to jail.

There are depositions in this affair which mention, that several guns were fired at the same time from the Custom-house; before which this shocking scene was exhibited. Into this matter inquisition is now making. In the meantime it may be proper to insert here the substance of some of those depositions.

Benjamin Frizell, on the evening of the 5th of March, having taken his station near the west corner of the Custom-house in King street, before and at the time of the soldiers firing their guns, declares (among other things) that the first discharge was only of one gun, the next of two guns, upon which he the deponent thinks he saw a man stumble; the third discharge was of three guns, upon which he thinks he saw two men fall; and immediately after were discharged five guns, two of which were by soldiers on his right hand; the other three, as appeared to the deponent, were discharged from the balcony, or the chamber window of the Custom-house, the flashes appearing on the left hand, and higher than the right hand flashes appeared to be, and of which the deponent was very sensible, although his eyes were much turned to the soldiers, who were all on his right hand.

What gave occasion to the melancholy event of that evening seems to have been this. A difference having happened near Mr. Grays ropewalk, between a soldier and a man belonging to it, the soldier challenged the ropemakers to a boxing match. The challenge was accepted by one of them, and the soldier worsted. He ran to the barrack in the neighborhood, and returned with several of his companions. The fray was renewed, and the soldiers were driven off. They soon returned with recruits and were again worsted. This happened several times, till at length a considerable body of soldiers was collected, and they also were driven off, the ropemakers having been joined by their brethren of the contiguous ropewalks. By this time Mr. Gray being alarmed interposed, and with the assistance of some gentlemen prevented any further disturbance. To satisfy the soldiers and punish the man who had been the occasion of the first difference, and as an example to the rest, he turned him out of his service; and waited on Col. Dalrymple, the commanding officer of the troops, and with him concerted measures for preventing further mischief. Though this affair ended thus, it made a strong impression on the minds of the soldiers in general, who thought the honor of the regiment concerned to revenge those repeated repulses. For this purpose they seem to have formed a combination to commit some outrage upon the inhabitants of the town indiscriminately; and this was to be done on the evening of the 5th instant or soon after; as appears by the depositions of the following persons, viz.:

William Newhall declares, that on Thursday night the 1st of March instant, he met four soldiers of the 29th regiment, and that he heard them say, "there were a great many that would eat their dinners on Monday next, that should not eat any on Tuesday."

Daniel Calfe declares, that on Saturday evening the 3d of March, a camp-woman, wife to James McDeed, a grenadier of the 29th, came into his father's shop, and the people talking about the affrays at the ropewalks, and blaming the soldiers for the part they had acted in it, the woman said, "the soldiers were in the right;" adding, "that before Tuesday or Wednesday night they would wet their swords or bayonets in New England people's blood."

Samuel Drowne declares that, about nine o'clock of the evening of the fifth of March current, standing at his own door in Cornhill, he saw about fourteen or fifteen soldiers of the 29th regiment, who came from Murray's barracks, armed with naked cutlasses and swords and came upon the inhabitants of the town, then standing or walking in Cornhill, and abused some, and violently assaulted others as they met them; most of whom were without so much as a stick in their hand to defend themselves, as he very clearly could discern, it being moonlight, and himself being one of the assaulted persons. All or most of the said soldiers he saw go into King street (some of them through Royal Exchange lane), and there followed them, and soon discovered them to be quarrelling and fighting with the people whom they saw there, which he thinks were not more than a dozen, when the soldiers came first, armed as aforesaid. Of those dozen people, the most of them were gentlemen, standing together a little below the Town House, upon the Exchange. At the appearance of those soldiers so armed, the most of the twelve persons went off, some of them being first assaulted.

The violent proceedings of this party, and their going into King street, "quarrelling and fighting with the people whom they saw there" (mentioned in Mr. Drowne's deposition), was immediately introductory to the grand catastrophe.

These assailants, who issued from Murray's barracks (so called), after attacking and wounding divers persons in Cornhill, as above mentioned, being armed, proceeded (most of them) up the Royal Exchange lane into King street; where, making a short stop, and after assaulting and driving away the few they met there, they brandished their arms and cried out, "where are the boogers! where are the cowards!" At this time there were very few persons in the street beside themselves. This party in proceeding from Exchange lane into King street, must pass the sentry posted at the westerly corner of the Custom House, which butts on that lane and fronts on that street. This is needful to be mentioned, as near that spot and in that street the bloody tragedy was acted, and the street actors in it were stationed: their station being but a few feet from the front side of the said Custom House. The outrageous behavior and the threats of the said party occasioned the ringing of the meeting-house bell near the head of King street, which bell ringing quick, as for fire, it presently brought out a number of inhabitants, who being soon sensible of the occasion of it, were naturally led to King street, where the said party had made a stop but a little while before, and where their stopping had drawn together a number of boys, round the sentry at the Custom House. whether the boys mistook the sentry for one of the said party, and thence took occasion to differ with him, or whether he first affronted them, which is affirmed in several depositions, however that may be, there was much foul language between them, and some of them, in consequence of his pushing at them with his bayonet, threw snowballs at him, which occasioned him to knock hastily at the door of the Custom House. From hence two persons thereupon proceeded immediately to the main-guard, which was posted opposite to the State House, at a small distance, near the head of the said street. The officer on guard was Capt. Preston, who with seven or eight soldiers, with fire-arms and charged bayonets, issued from the guardhouse, and in great haste posted himself and his soldiers in front of the Custom House, near the corner aforesaid. In passing to this station the soldiers pushed several persons with their bayonets, driving through the people in so rough a manner that it appeared they intended to create a disturbance. This occasioned some snowballs to be thrown at them which seems to have been the only provocation that was given. Mr. Knox (between whom and Capt. Preston there was some conversation on the spot) declares, that while he was talking with Capt. Preston, the soldiers of his detachment had attacked the people with their bayonets and that there was not the least provocation given to Capt. Preston of his party; the backs of the people being toward them when the people were attacked. He also declares, that Capt. Preston seemed to be in great haste and much agitated, and that, according to his opinion, there were not then present in King street above seventy or eighty persons at the extent.

The said party was formed into a half circle; and within a short time after they had been posted at the Custom House, began to fire upon the people.

Captain Preston is said to have ordered them to fire, and to have repeated that order. One gun was fired first; then others in succession and with deliberation, till ten or a dozen guns were fired; or till that number of discharges were made from the guns that were fired. By which means eleven persons were killed and wounded, as above represented.

(A Short Narrative of the Horrid Massacre in Boston. Printed by Order of the Town of Boston. Re-published with Notes and Illustrations by John Doggett, Jr., (New York, 1849), vp. 13-19; 21- 22; 28-30.)

Boston Massacre from British Point of View:

Captain Thomas Preston's account of the Boston Massacre, 13 March 1770

It is [a] matter of too great notoriety to need any proofs that the arrival of his Majesty's troops in Boston was extremely obnoxious to its inhabitants. They have ever used all means in their power to weaken the regiments, and to bring them into contempt by promoting and aiding desertions, and with impunity, even where there has been the clearest evidence of the fact, and by grossly and falsely propagating untruths concerning them. On the arrival of the 64th and 65th their ardour seemingly began to abate; it being too expensive to buy off so many, and attempts of that kind rendered too dangerous from the numbers

And has ever since their departure been breaking out with greater violence after their embarkation. One of their justices, most thoroughly acquainted with the people and their intentions, on the trial of a man of the 14th Regiment, openly and publicly in the hearing of great numbers of people and from the seat of justice, declared "that the soldiers must now take care of themselves, nor trust too much to their arms, for they were but a handful; that the inhabitants carried weapons concealed under their clothes, and would destroy them in a moment, if they pleased". This, considering the malicious temper of the people, was an alarming circumstance to the soldiery. Since which several disputes have happened between the townspeople and the soldiers of both regiments, the former being encouraged thereto by the countenance of even some of the magistrates, and by the protection of all the party against government. In general such disputes have been kept too secret from the officers. On the 2nd instant two of the 29th going through one Gray's ropewalk, the ropemakers insultingly asked them if they would empty a vault. This unfortunately had the desired effect by provoking the soldiers, and from words they went to blows. Both parties suffered in this affair, and finally the soldiers retired to their quarters. The officers, on the first knowledge of this transaction, took every precaution in their power to prevent any ill consequence. Notwithstanding which, single quarrels could not be prevented, the inhabitants constantly provoking and abusing the soldiery. The insolence as well as utter hatred of the inhabitants to the troops increased daily, insomuch that Monday and Tuesday, the 5th and 6th instant, were privately agreed on for a general engagement, in consequence of which several of the militia came from the country armed to join their friends, menacing to destroy any who should oppose them. This plan has since been discovered.

On Monday night about 8 o'clock two soldiers were attacked and beat. But the party of the townspeople in order to carry matters to the utmost length, broke into two meeting houses and rang the alarm bells, which I supposed was for fire as usual, but was soon undeceived. About 9 some of the guard came to and informed me the town inhabitants were assembling to attack the troops, and that the bells were ringing as the signal for that purpose and not for fire, and the beacon intended to be fired to bring in the distant people of the country. This, as I was captain of the day, occasioned my repairing immediately to the main guard. In my way there I saw the people in great commotion, and heard them use the most cruel and horrid threats against the troops. In a few minutes after I reached the guard, about 100 people passed it and went towards the custom house where the king's money is lodged. They immediately surrounded the sentry posted there, and with clubs and other weapons threatened to execute their vengeance on him. I was soon informed by a townsman their intention was to carry off the soldier from his post and probably murder him. On which I desired him to return for further intelligence, and he soon came back and assured me he heard the mob declare they would murder him. This I feared might be a prelude to their plundering the king's chest. I immediately sent a non-commissioned officer and 12 men to protect both the sentry and the king's money, and very soon followed myself to prevent, if possible, all disorder, fearing lest the officer and soldiers, by the insults and provocations of the rioters, should be thrown off their guard and commit some rash act. They soon rushed through the people, and by charging their bayonets in half-circles, kept them at a little distance. Nay, so far was I from intending the death of any person that I suffered the troops to go to the spot where the unhappy affair took place without any loading in their pieces; nor did I ever give orders for loading them. This remiss conduct in me perhaps merits censure; yet it is evidence, resulting from the nature of things, which is the best and surest that can be offered, that my intention was not to act offensively, but the contrary part, and that not without compulsion. The mob still increased and were more outrageous, striking their clubs or bludgeons one against another, and calling out, come on you rascals, you bloody backs, you lobster scoundrels, fire if you dare, xxxx, fire and be damned, we know you dare not, and much more such language was used. At this time I was between the soldiers and the mob, parleying with, and endeavouring all in my power to persuade them to retire peaceably, but to no purpose. They advanced to the points of the bayonets, struck some of them and even the muzzles of the pieces, and seemed to be endeavouring to close with the soldiers. On which some well behaved persons asked me if the guns were charged. I replied yes. They then asked me if I intended to order the men to fire. I answered no, by no means, observing to them that I was advanced before the muzzles of the men's pieces, and must fall a sacrifice if they fired; that the soldiers were upon the half and charged bayonets, and my giving the word fire under those circumstances would prove me to be no officer. While I was thus speaking, one of the soldiers having received a severe blow with a stick, stepped a little on one side and instantly fired, on which turning to and asking him why he fired without orders, I was struck with a club on my arm, which for some time deprived me of the use of it, which blow had it been placed on my head, most probably would have destroyed me.

On this a general attack was made on the men by a great number of heavy clubs and snowballs being thrown at them, by which all our lives were in imminent danger, some persons at the same time from behind calling out, damn your bloods-why don't you fire. Instantly three or four of the soldiers fired, one after another, and directly after three more in the same confusion and hurry. The mob then ran away, except three unhappy men who instantly expired, in which number was Mr. Gray at whose rope-walk the prior quarrels took place; one more is since dead, three others are dangerously, and four slightly wounded. The whole of this melancholy affair was transacted in almost 20 minutes. On my asking the soldiers why they fired without orders, they said they heard the word fire and supposed it came from me. This might be the case as many of the mob called out fire, fire, but I assured the men that I gave no such order; that my words were, don't fire, stop your firing. In short, it was scarcely possible for the soldiers to know who said fire, or don't fire, or stop your firing. On the people's assembling again to take away the dead bodies, the soldiers supposing them coming to attack them, were making ready to fire again, which I prevented by striking up their firelocks with my hand. Immediately after a townsman came and told me that 4 or 5000 people were assembled in the next street, and had sworn to take my life with every man's with me. On which I judged it unsafe to remain there any longer, and therefore sent the party and sentry to the main guard, where the street is narrow and short, there telling them off into street firings, divided and planted them at each end of the street to secure their rear, momentarily expecting an attack, as there was a constant cry of the inhabitants to arms, to arms, turn out with your guns; and the town drums beating to arms, I ordered my drums to beat to arms, and being soon after joined by the different companies of the 29th regiment, I formed them as the guard into street firings. The 14th regiment also got under arms but remained at their barracks. I immediately sent a sergeant with a party to Colonel Dalrymple, the commanding officer, to acquaint him with every particular. Several officers going to join their regiment were knocked down by the mob, one very much wounded and his sword taken from him. The lieutenant-governor and Colonel Carr soon after met at the head of the 29th regiment and agreed that the regiment should retire to their barracks, and the people to their houses, but I kept the picket to strengthen the guard. It was with great difficulty that the lieutenant-governor prevailed on the people to be quiet and retire. At last they all went off, excepting about a hundred.

A Council was immediately called, on the breaking up of which three justices met and issued a warrant to apprehend me and eight soldiers. On hearing of this procedure I instantly went to the sheriff and surrendered myself, though for the space of 4 hours I had it in my power to have made my escape, which I most undoubtedly should have attempted and could easily executed, had I been the least conscious of any guilt. On the examination before the justices, two witnesses swore that I gave the men orders to fire. The one testified he was within two feet of me; the other that I swore at the men for not firing at the first word. Others swore they heard me use the word "fire," but whether do or do not fire, they could not say; others that they heard the word fire, but could not say if it came from me. The next day they got 5 or 6 more to swear I gave the word to fire. So bitter and inveterate are many of the malcontents here that they are industriously using every method to fish out evidence to prove it was a concerted scheme to murder the inhabitants. Others are infusing the utmost malice and revenge into the minds of the people who are to be my jurors by false publications, votes of towns, and all other artifices. That so from a settled rancor against the officers and troops in general, the suddenness of my trial after the affair while the people's minds are all greatly inflamed, I am, though perfectly innocent, under most unhappy circumstances, having nothing in reason to expect but the loss of life in a very ignominious manner, without the interposition of his Majesty's royal goodness.

(Captain Thomas Preston's Account of the Boston Massacre (13 march 1770), from British Public Records Office, C. O. 5/759. Reprinted in Merrill Jensen (editor) English Historical Documents, Volume IX. (London, 1964) vp. 750-53.)

"The Way to Wealth" by Benjamin Franklin

In 1732, I first published my Almanac under the name of Richard Saunders; it was continued by me about twenty-five years, and commonly called *Poor Richard's Almanac*. I endeavoured to make it both entertaining and useful, and it accordingly came to be in such demand, that I reaped considerable profit from it, vending annually near ten thousand. And observing that it was generally read, (scarce any neigbbourbood in the province being without it,) I considered it as a proper vehicle for conveying instruction among the common people, who bought Scarcely any other books. I therefore filled all the little spaces, that occurred between the remarkable days in the Calendar, with proverbial sentences, chiefly such as inculcated industry and frugality, as the means of procuring wealth, and thereby securing virtue; it being more difficult for a man in want to act always honestly, as (to use here one of those proverbs) It is hard for an empty sack to stand upright"

The Way to Wealth COURTEOUS Reader,
I have heard that nothing gives an author so great pleasure as to find his works respectfully quoted by others. Judge, then, how much I must have been gratified by an incident I am going to relate to you. I stopped my horse lately, where a great number of people were collected at an auction of merchants' goods. The hour of the sale not being come, they were conversing on the badness of the times; and one of the company called to a plain, clean old man, with white locks, "Pray, Father Abraham, what think you of the times? Will not these heavy taxes quite ruin the country? How shall we ever be able to pay them? What would you advise us to do?" Father Abraham stood, up and replied, "If you would have my advice, I will give it you in short; for A word to the wise is enough, as Poor Richard says." They joined in desiring him to speak his mind, and gathering round him he proceeded as follows.

"Friends," said he, "the taxes are indeed very heavy, and, if those laid on by the government were the only ones we had to pay, we might more easily discharge them; but we have many others, and much more grievous to some of us. We are taxed twice as much by our idleness, three times as much by our pride, and four times as much by our folly; and from these taxes the commissioners cannot ease or deliver us by allowing an abatement. However, let us hearken to good advice, and something maybe done for us; God helps them that help themselves, as Poor Richard says.

"I. It would be thought a hard government that should tax its people one-tenth part of their time, to be employed in its service; but idleness taxes many of us much more; sloth, by bringing on diseases, absolutely shortens life. Sloth, like rust, consumes faster than labor wears; while the used key is always bright, as Poor Richard says. But dost thou love life, then do not squander time, for that is the stuff life is made of, as Poor Richard says. How much more than is necessary do we spend in sleep, forgetting, that The sleeping fox catches no poultry, and that, There will be sleeping enough in the grave, as Poor Richard says.

"If time be of all things the most precious, wasting time must be, as Poor Richard says, the greatest prodigality; since, as he elsewhere tells us, Lost time is never found again; and what we call time enough, always proves little enough. Let us, then, up and be doing, and doing to the purpose; so by diligence shall we do more with less perplexity. Sloth makes all things difficult, but industry all easy; and He that riseth late must trot all day, and shall scarce overtake his business at night; while Laziness travels so slowly, that Poverty soon overtakes him. Drive thy business, let not that drive thee; and Early to bed, and early to rise, makes a man healthy, wealthy, and wise, as Poor Richard says.

"Methinks I hear some of you say, `Must a man afford himself no leisure?' I will tell thee, my friend, what Poor Richard says, Employ thy time well, if thou meanest to gain leisure; and, since thou art not sure of a minute, throw not away an hour. Leisure is time for doing something useful; this leisure the diligent man will obtain, but the lazy man never; for A life of leisure and a life of laziness are two things. Many, without labor, would live by their wits only, but they break for want of stock; whereas industry gives comfort, and plenty, and respect. Fly pleasures, and they will follow you. The diligent spinner has a large shift; and now I have a sheep and a cow, everybody bids me good morrow.

"II. But with our industry we must likewise be steady, settled, and careful, and oversee our own affairs with our own eye, and not too much to others; for, as Poor Richard says,

I never saw an oft-removed tree,
Nor yet an oft-removed family,
That throve so well as those that settled be.

And again, Three removes are as bad as a fire; and again, Keep thy shop, and thy shop will keep thee; and again, If you would have your business done, go; if not, send. And again,

He that by the plough would thrive,
Himself must either hold or drive.

And again, The eye of a master will do more work than both his hands; and again, Want of care does us more damage than want of knowledge; and again, Not to oversee workmen, is to leave them your purse open. Trusting too much to others' care is the ruin of many; for In the affairs of this world men are saved, not by faith, but by the want of it; but a man's own care is profitable; for, If you would have a faithful servant, and one that you like, serve yourself. A little neglect may breed great mischief; for want of a nail the shoe was lost; for want of a shoe the horse was lost; and for want of a horse the rider was lost, being overtaken and slain by the enemy; all for want of a little care about a horse-shoe nail.

"III. So much for industry, my friends, and attention to one's own business; but to these we must add frugality, if we would make our industry more certainly successful. A man may, if he knows not how to save as he gets, keep his nose all his life to the grindstone, and die not worth a groat at last. A fat kitchen makes a lean will; and

Many estate are spent in the getting,
Since women for tea forsook spinning and knitting,
And men for punch forsook hewing and splitting.

If you would be wealthy, think of saving as well as of getting. The Indies have not made Spain rich, because her outgoes are greater than her incomes.

"Away, then, with your expensive follies, and you will not then have so much cause to complain of hard times, heavy taxes, and chargeable families; for

Women and wine, game and deceit,
Make the wealth small and the want great.

And further, What maintains one vice would bring up two children. You may think, perhaps, that a little tea, or a little punch now and then, diet a little more costly, clothes a little finer, and a little entertainment now and then, can be no great matter; but remember, Many a little makes a mickle. Beware of little expenses; A small leak will sink a great ship, as Poor Richard says; and again, Who dainties love, shall beggars prove; and moreover, Fools make feasts. and wise men eat them. . . . If you would know the value of money, go and try to borrow some; for he that goes a borrowing goes a sorrowing, as Poor Richard says; and indeed so does he that lends to such people, when he goes to get it in again. Poor Dick further advises, and says,

Fond pride of drew is sure a very curse;
Ere fancy you consult, consult your purse.

And again, Pride is as loud a beggar as Want, and a great deal more saucy. When you have bought one fine thing, you must buy ten more, that your appearance may be all of a piece; but Poor Dick says. It is easier to suppress the first desire, than to satisfy all that follow it. And, it is as truly folly for the poor to ape the rich, as for the frog to swell in order to equal the ox.

Vessels large may venture more,
But little boats should keep near shore.

It is, however, a folly soon punished; for, as Poor Richard says, Pride that dines on vanity, sups on contempt. Pride breakfasted with Plenty, dined with Poverty, and supped with Infamy. And, after all, of what use is this pride of appearance, for which so much is risked, so much is suffered? It cannot promote health, nor ease pain; it makes no increase of merit in the person; it creates envy; it hastens misfortune.

"But what madness must it be to run in debt for these superfluities. When you have got your bargain, you may, perhaps, think little of payment; but, as Poor Richard says, Creditors have better memories than debtors; creditors are a superstitious sect, great observers of set days and times. The day comes round before you are aware, and the demand is made before you are prepared to satisfy it; or, if you bear your debt in mind, the term, which at first seemed so long, will, as it lessens, appear extremely short. Time will seem to have added wings to his heels as well as his shoulders. Those have a short Lent, who owe money to be paid at Easter. At present, perhaps, you may think yourselves in thriving circumstances, and that you can bear a little extravagance without injury; but

For age and want save while you may;
No morning sun lasts a whole day.

Gain may be temporary and uncertain, but ever, while you live, expense is constant and certain; and It is easier to build two chimneys, than to keep one in fuel, as Poor Richard says; so, Rather go to bed supperless, than in debt.

Get what you can, and what you get hold;
'Tis the stone that will turn all your lead into gold.

And when you have got the Philosopher's stone, sure you will no longer complain of bad times, or the difficulty of paying taxes.

"IV. This doctrine, my friends, is reason and wisdom; but, after do not depend too much upon your own industry, and frugality, and prudence, though excellent things; for they may all be blasted, without the blessing of Heaven; and, therefore, ask that blessing humbly, and be not uncharitable to those that at present seem to want it, but comfort and help them. Remember, Job suffered, and was afterward prosperous.

"And now, to conclude, Experience keeps a dear school, but fools will learn in no other, as Poor Richard says, and scarce in that; for, it is true, We may give advice, but we cannot give conduct. However, remember this, They that will not be counselled, cannot be helped; and further, that, If you will not hear Reason, she will surely rap your knuckles, as Poor Richard says."

Thus the old gentleman ended his harangue. The people heard it and approved the doctrine; and immediately practised the contrary, just as if it had been a common sermon; for the auction opened, and they began to buy extravagantly. I found the good man had thoroughly studied my Almanacs, and digested all I had dropped on these topics during the course of twenty-five years. The frequent mention he made of me must have tired any one else; but my vanity was wonderfully delighted with it, though I was conscious that not a tenth part of the wisdom was my own, which he ascribed to me, but rather the gleanings that I had made of the sense of all ages and nations. However, I resolved to be the better for the echo of it; and though I had at first determined to buy stuff for a new coat, I went away resolved to wear my old one a little longer. Reader, if thou wilt do the same, thy profit will be as great as mine. I am, as ever, thine to serve thee,

RICHARD SAUNDERS.

The End

The Bill of Rights

Amendments 1-10 of the United States Constitution

The Conventions of a number of the States having, at the time of adopting the Constitution, expressed a desire, in order to prevent misconstruction or abuse of its powers, that further declaratory and restrictive clauses should be added, and as extending the ground of public confidence in the Government will best insure the beneficent ends of its institution;

Resolved, by the Senate and House of Representatives of the United States of America, in Congress assembled, two-thirds of both Houses concurring, that the following articles be proposed to the Legislatures of the several States, as amendments to the Constitution of the United States; all or any of which articles, when ratified by three-fourths of the said Legislatures, to be valid to all intents and purposes as part of the said Constitution, namely:

Amendment I
Congress shall make no law respecting an establishment of religion, or prohibiting the free exercise thereof; or abridging the freedom of speech, or of the press; or the right of the people peaceably to assemble, and to petition the government for a redress of grievances.

Amendment II
A well regulated militia, being necessary to the security of a free state, the right of the people to keep and bear arms, shall not be infringed.

Amendment III
No soldier shall, in time of peace be quartered in any house, without the consent of the owner, nor in time of war, but in a manner to be prescribed by law.

Amendment IV
The right of the people to be secure in their persons, houses, papers, and effects, against unreasonable searches and seizures, shall not be violated, and no warrants shall issue, but upon probable cause, supported by oath or affirmation, and particularly describing the place to be searched, and the persons or things to be seized.

Amendment V
No person shall be held to answer for a capital, or otherwise infamous crime, unless on a presentment or indictment of a grand jury, except in cases arising in the land or naval forces, or in the militia, when in actual service in time of war or public danger; nor shall any person be subject for the same offense to be twice put in jeopardy of life or limb; nor shall be compelled in any criminal case to be a witness against himself, nor be deprived of life, liberty, or property, without due process of law; nor shall private property be taken for public use, without just compensation.

Amendment VI
In all criminal prosecutions, the accused shall enjoy the right to a speedy and public trial, by an impartial jury of the state and district wherein the crime shall have been committed, which district shall have

been previously ascertained by law, and to be informed of the nature and cause of the accusation; to be confronted with the witnesses against him; to have compulsory process for obtaining witnesses in his favor, and to have the assistance of counsel for his defense.

Amendment VII
In suits at common law, where the value in controversy shall exceed twenty dollars, the right of trial by jury shall be preserved, and no fact tried by a jury, shall be otherwise reexamined in any court of the United States, than according to the rules of the common law.

Amendment VIII
Excessive bail shall not be required, nor excessive fines imposed, nor cruel and unusual punishments inflicted.

Amendment IX
The enumeration in the Constitution, of certain rights, shall not be construed to deny or disparage others retained by the people.

Amendment X
The powers not delegated to the United States by the Constitution, nor prohibited by it to the states, are reserved to the states respectively, or to the people.

APPENDIX L

Excerpts from the Age of Reason and the Enlightenment

SELECTIONS FROM *OF CIVIL GOVERNMENT* (1690) by John Locke

The State of Nature: To understand political power aright, we must consider what state all men are naturally in, and that is, a state of perfect freedom to order their actions and dispose of their possessions and persons, as they think fit, within the bounds of the law of nature; without asking leave, or depending upon the will of any other man. . . .The state of nature has a law of nature to govern it, which obliges every one: and reason, which is that law, teaches all mankind, that being all equal and independent, no one ought to harm another in his life, health, liberty, or possessions: for men [are] all the workmanship of one omnipotent and infinitely wise Maker; all the servants of one sovereign master, sent into the world by his order, and about his business. . . .

Reason: Men living together according to reason, without a common superior on earth, with authority to judge between them, is properly the state of nature. God, who hath given the world to men in common, hath also given them reason to make use of it to the best advantage of life, and convenience. The earth, and all that is therein, is given to men for the support and comfort of their being. Nothing was made by God for man to spoil or destroy. And thus, considering the plenty of natural provision there was a long time in the world, and the few spenders . . there could be then little room for quarrels or contentions about property so established.

SELECTIONS FROM *COMMON SENSE* (1776) by Thomas Paine

Society in every state is a blessing, but government even in its best state is but a necessary evil in its worst state an in tolerable one; for when we suffer, or are exposed to the same miseries by a government, which we might expect in a country without government, our calamities is heightened by reflecting that we furnish the means by which we suffer! Government, like dress, is the badge of lost innocence; the palaces of kings are built on the ruins of the bowers of paradise. For were the impulses of conscience clear, uniform, and irresistibly obeyed, man would need no other lawgiver; but that not being the case, he finds it necessary to surrender up a part of his property to furnish means for the protection of the rest; and this he is induced to do by the same prudence which in every other case advises him out of two evils to choose the least. Wherefore, security being the true design and end of government, it unanswerably follows that whatever form thereof appears most likely to ensure it to us, with the least expense and greatest benefit, is preferable to all others.

SELECTIONS FROM *THE AMERICAN CRISIS* (1776) by Thomas Paine

THESE are the times that try men's souls. The summer soldier and the sunshine patriot will, in this crisis, shrink from the service of their country; but he that stands it now, deserves the love and thanks of man and woman. Tyranny, like hell, is not easily conquered; yet we have this consolation with us, that the harder the conflict, the more glorious the triumph. What we obtain too cheap, we esteem too lightly: it is dearness only that gives every thing its value. Heaven knows how to put a proper price upon its goods; and it would be strange indeed if so celestial an article as FREEDOM should not be highly rated. Britain, with an army to enforce her tyranny, has declared that she has a right (not only to TAX) but "to BIND us in ALL CASES WHATSOEVER," and if being bound in that manner, is not slavery, then is there not such a thing as slavery upon earth.

SELECTIONS FROM "THE SPIRIT OF THE LAWS" (1749) by Charles de Secondat, Baron de Montesquieu

Of the Laws in General: Laws, in their most general meaning, are the necessary relations arising from the nature of things. In this sense, all beings have their laws, the Deity his laws, the material world its laws, the intelligences superior to man their laws, the beasts their laws, man his laws. . . . Since we observe that the world, though formed by the motion of matter, and void of understanding, subsists through so long a succession of ages, its motions must certainly be directed by invariable laws. . . . Law in general is human reason, inasmuch as it governs all the inhabitants of the earth; the political and civil laws of each nation ought to be only the particular cases in which human reason is applied. They should be adapted in this manner to the people for whom they are framed, because it is most unlikely that the laws of one nation will suit another. They should be relative to the nature and principle of each government. . . . They should be relative to the climate of each country, to the quality of its soil, to its situation and extent, to the principal occupation of the inhabitants, whether farmers, huntsmen, or shepherds: they should have a relation to the degree of liberty which the constitution will bear, to the religion of the inhabitants, to their manners, and customs . . . in all which different respects they ought to be considered.

Of Political Liberty and the Constitution of England: Political liberty is to be found only in moderate governments; and even in these it is not always found. It is there only when there is no abuse of power: but constant experience shows us that every man invested with power is apt to abuse it, and to carry his authority as far as it will go. To prevent this abuse, it is necessary, from the very nature of things, that power should be a check to power. The political liberty of the subject is a tranquility of mind arising from the opinion each person has of his safety. In order to have this liberty, it is requisite the government be so constituted as one man need not be afraid of another. When the legislative and executive powers are united in the same person, or in the same body of magistrates, there can be no liberty. . . . Again, there is no liberty if the judiciary power be not separated from the legislative and executive. In perusing the admirable treatise of Tacitus on the manners of the ancient German tribes, we find it is from that nation the English have borrowed the idea of their political government. This beautiful system was invented first in the woods. . . . Neither do I pretend by this to undervalue other governments, nor to say that this extreme political liberty ought to give uneasiness to those who have only a moderate share of it. How should I have any such design; I who think that even the highest refinement of reason is not always desirable, and that mankind generally find their account better in mediums than in extremes?

(Source: Montesquieu, Charles de Secondat, Baron de. *The Complete Works of M. de Montesquieu*. London: T. Evans and W. Davis, 1777)

SELECTIONS FROM *THE SOCIAL CONTRACT* (1762) by Jean Jacques Rousseau

Man is born free, and everywhere he is in chains. Many a one believes himself the master of others, and yet he is a greater slave than they. . . . The social order is a sacred right which serves as a foundation for all others . . . now, as men cannot create any new forces, but only combine and direct those that exist, they have no other means of self-preservation than to form...a sum of forces which may overcome the resistance, to put them in action and to make them work in concert. This sum of forces can be produced only by the combination of man; but the strength and freedom of each man being the chief instruments of his preservation, how can he pledge them without injuring himself, and without neglecting the cares which he owes to himself? This difficulty, applied to my subject, may be expressed in these terms:

To find a form of association which may defend and protect with the whole force of the community the person and property of all its members and by means of which each, coalescing with all, may nevertheless obey only himself, and remain as free as before. Such is the fundamental problem of which the social contract furnishes the solution.

In short, each giving himself to all, gives himself to nobody. . . We see from this formula that the act of association contains a reciprocal engagement between the public and individuals, and that every individual . . . is engaged in a double relation. . . . the social pact . . . includes this engagement . . . that whoever refuses to obey the general will shall be constrained to do so by the whole body; which means nothing else than that he shall be forced to be free. . . .

(Source: Rousseau, *The Social Contract*, Henry J. Tozer, trans., London, 1895)

APPENDIX M

"The Two Grenadiers"

"The Two Grenadiers" tells the story of two French soldiers captured by the Russians, one of whom dreams of fighting for his Emperor (Napoleon) from the grave.

Two grenadiers were returning to France,
From Russian captivity they came.
And as they crossed into German lands
They hung their heads in shame.

Both heard there the tale that they dreaded most,
That France had been conquered in war;
Defeated and shattered, that once proud host,
And the Emperor, a free man no more.

The grenadiers both started to weep
At hearing so sad a review.
The first said, "My pain is too deep;
My old wound is burning anew!"

The other said, "The song is done;
Like you, I'd not stay alive;
But at home I have wife and son,
Who without me would not survive."

What matters son? What matters wife?
By nobler needs I set store;
Let them go beg to sustain their life!
My Emperor, a free man no more!

Promise me, brother, one request:
If at this time I should die,
Take my corpse to France for its final rest;
In France's dear earth let me lie.

The Cross of Valor, on its red band,
Over my heart you shall lay;
My musket place into my hand;
And my sword at my side display.

So shall I lie and hark in the ground,
A guardwatch, silently staying
Till once more I hear the cannon's pound
And the hoofbeats of horses neighing.

Then my Emperor'll be passing right over my grave;
Each clashing sword, a flashing reflector.
And I, fully armed, will rise up from that grave,
The Emperor's, the Emperor's protector!"

(Translation from German to English copyright © 1995 by Walter Meyer)

APPENDIX N

Recommended Resources

Scotland and England

Austen, Jane. *Pride and Prejudice*.

—*Sense and Sensibility*.

Defoe, Daniel. *Robinson Crusoe*. Considered the first English novel.

Sutcliff, Rosemary. *Bonnie Dundee*. Peter Smith, 1990. Historical fiction. An adventure story set in Scotland during the war between King James and William, featuring a 17-year-old hero.

—*Flame-Colored Taffeta*. Farrar, 1986. Historical fiction. A young girl helps a wounded smuggler in this story set in 18th-century England.

Slavery and Africa

Collier, James and Christopher. *Jump Ship to Freedom*. Yearling, 1987. Historical fiction. Daniel is a 13-year-old slave living in Connecticut. His father is fighting in the War of Independence while he and his mother are taken to the West Indies to be sold.

Davidson, Basil. *The African Slave Trade*. Little, Brown, 1988. Details of four centuries of African slave trade.

—*The Lost Cities of Africa*. Little, Brown, 1988. The history and culture of Africa before the arrival of Europeans.

Douglass, Frederick. *Narrative of the Life of Frederick Douglass, an American Slave*. This important primary source account of slavery is very graphic and not appropriate for young children.

Fox, Paula. *The Slave Dancer*. Laurel Leaf, 1997. Historical fiction. A teenage boy becomes an indentured servant aboard a slave ship. He is forced to play music so the slaves will "dance" and look strong at the market.

Gaeddert, Louann. *Breaking Free*. Historical fiction. Set in New York during 1800, a 12-year-old boy secretly teaches a young slave to read and helps her escape to Canada.

Jones, Constance. *A Short History of Africa: 1500-1900*. Facts on File, 1993.

Killingray, David. *The Transatlantic Slave Trade*. Batsford, 1987. Detailed coverage of the causes, history, and end of the international slave trade.

Lester, Julius. *To Be a Slave*. New York: Scholastic, 1968. Stories told by men and women who lived through slavery. A Newbery Honor winner.

O'Dell, Scott. *My Name Is Not Angelica*. Houghton, 1979. Historical fiction. The story of an African girl who is taken as a slave to the Danish Virgin Islands.

Stowe, Harriet Beecher. *Uncle Tom's Cabin or, Life Among the Lowly*.

Wyeth, Sharon D. *Once on This River*. New York: Knopf, 1997. Historical fiction set in an African American community in New York in 1760. A young girl learns her mother gave her away so she could be free.

Pirates

Avi. *Captain Grey*. HarperCollins, 1993. Historical fiction. An adventure story of a young boy kidnapped by pirates. Takes place in 18th-century Philadelphia.

Beahm, George. *Caribbean Pirates: A Treasure Chest of Fact, Fiction, and Folklore*. Hampton Roads Pub Co., 2007. Informative book that separates pirate fact from Hollywood fiction.

Pirate (DK Eyewitness Book). DK Children, 2004.

Stevenson, Robert Louis. *Treasure Island*.

Scientific Revolution

Hakim, Joy. *The Story of Science: Newton At the Center*. Washington: Smithsonian Books, 2005. Part science, part history. Covers all the major players in the Scientific Revolution.

Rosen, Sydney. *Galileo and the Magic Numbers*. Little Brown & Co., 1958.

Industrial Revolution

Cahn, Rhoda and William. *No Time for School, No Time for Play*. New York: Julian Messner, 1972

Corrick, James A. *The Industrial Revolution*. Lucent, 1998.

Dickens, Charles. *Hard Times*. New York: Bantam Books: 1964.

Hakim, Joy. *The Age of Extremes*. New York: Oxford University Press, 1994.

— *The History of Us: Reconstruction and Reform*. New York: Oxford University Press, 1994.

— *The New Nation*. New York: Oxford University Press, 1993.

Langley, Andrew. *The Industrial Revolution*. New York: Viking, 1994.

McCormick, Anita Louise. *The Industrial Revolution in American History*. Springfield: Enslow Publishers, Inc., 1998.

Rutherford, Edward. *London*. Crown, 1997. A lengthy novel that traces the history of London through he eyes of families throughout the ages.

APPENDIX N

Wilkerson, Philip, and Jacqueline Dineen. *The Industrial Revolution*. Chelsea, 1995.

The Enlightenment

Dunn, John M. *The Enlightenment*. Lucent, 1998.

Spencer, Lloyd. *Introducing the Enlightenment*. Totem, 1997.

France and Spain

Cervantes, Miquel de. *Don Quixote*. Classic literature set in 17th century Spain.

Dickens, Charles. *A Tale of Two Cities*. Classic literature about London and Paris during the French Revolution.

Dumas, Alexandre. *The Three Musketeers*. Classic literature set in 1625 France at the time of Cardinal Richelieu and Queen Anne of Austria.

Greene, Carol. *Simon Bolivar: South American Liberator*. Children's Press, 1989.

Orczy, Baroness. *The Scarlet Pimpernel*. Classic literature that takes place when the Reign of Terror grips France during the French Revolution and the time of the guillotine.

Henderson, Harry. *The Age of Napoleon*. Lucent, 1998.

Pietrusza, David. *The Battle of Waterloo*. Lucent, 1996. The story of the last battle of the Napoleonic Wars, includes maps, graphics, and timelines.

Sommerville, Donald. *Revolutionary and Napoleonic Wars*. Raintree Steck-Vaughn, 1998.

Wheeler, Thomas Gerald. *A Fanfare for the Stalwart*. Phillips, 1967. Historical fiction. An injured Frenchman is left behind when Napoleon retreats from Russia.

Native Americans and European Settlement of America

Blos, Joan W. A *Gathering of Days: A New England Girl's Journal 1830-32.* New York: Aladdin, 1990. Historical fiction set in Colonial America.

Boone, Daniel and Francis Lister Hawkes. *Daniel Boone*. Autobiography originally published in 1844.

Brink, Carol Ryrie. *Caddie Woodlawn*. Historical fiction set in Revolutionary America, Caddie's adventures in the Indian wilderness of Wisconsin.

Bulla, Clyde Robert. *A Lion to Guard Us*. New York: HarperTrophy, 1989. Historical fiction. Three kids travel from London to Jamestown.

Collier, James L. and Christopher Collier. *The Bloody Country*. Macmillan, 1985. Historical fiction. A pioneer story about a family that settles in Pennsylvania in the 1750s.

Conley, Robert. *War Woman: A Novel of the Real People*. St. Martin's, 1997. Fast-moving novel tells of first encounters between the Cherokees and Europeans.

Cousins, Margaret. *The Boy in the Alamo*. Corona Publishing Co., 1983. Historical fiction.

Crockett, David. *Davy Crockett: His Own Story*. This autobiography was originally written in 1834.

Farley, Karin Clafford. *Duel in the Wilderness*. George Washington as a general, based on his own journal.

Foster, Genevieve. *George Washington's World*. Biography of George Washington and those around him.

Grote, JoAnn A. *Queen Anne's War*. Chelsea, 1998. Historical fiction set in 1710 New England.

Harvey, Karen, ed. *American Indian Voices*. Millbrook, 1995. Thirty selections giving insight into the cultures and experiences of American Indians.

Kilian, Michael. *Major Washington*. St. Martin's, 1998. Historical fiction on the life of George Washington before he was President.

Lasky, Kathryn. *Beyond the Burning Time*. Scholastic, 1994. Docu-novel that captures the ignorance, violence, and hysteria of the Salem witch trials.

O'Dell, Scott. *Sing Down the Moon*. Houghton, 1970. Historical fiction. A young Navajo girl sees her culture destroyed by Spanish slavers and white soldiers.

—*The Serpent Never Sleeps: A Novel of Jamestown and Pocahontas*. Houghton, 1987.

Speare, Elizabeth George. *Calico Captive*. Houghton, 1957. Historical fiction. In Colonial America, a family is captured by Indians and the French during the French and Indian War, 1754.

Stewart, George Rippey. *The Pioneers Go West*. A gripping true story of 17-year-old Moses and his trip across the West to California in 1844.

Wisler, G. Clifton. *This New Land*. Walker, 1987. Historical fiction. A well-researched novel about a Pilgrim boy's adventures on the *Mayflower* and in the Plymouth Rock colony.

Wood, Nancy. *Thunderwoman*. Viking, 1998. This beautifully illustrated novel traces the history of the Pueblos and other peoples in the Western Hemisphere after 10,000 years of peace, beginning with the Spanish quests in the 1500s up to the atomic bomb testing in New Mexico.

The American Revolution

Avi. *Night Journeys*. HarperTrophy, 2000. Historical fiction. A 12-year-old orphan is adopted by a
Quaker family in pre-revolutionary Philadelphia.

Brady, Esther Wood. *Toliver's Secret*. Yearling, 1993. Historical fiction. The story of a girl who has to
sneak a message behind enemy lines during the War of Independence.

Collier, James L. *My Brother Sam is Dead*. Macmillan, 1974. Historical fiction. A young boy tells of the
tragic events leading to his brother's death in the Revolutionary War.

Fast, Howard. *April Morning*. Bantam Books, 1987. Historical fiction. The first days of the American
Revolution as experienced by a 15-year-old boy.

Herbert, Janis. *The American Revolution for Kids*. Chicago Review Press, 2002. Great activity book that's
filled with information.

Rinaldi, Ann. *The Fifth of March: A Story of the Boston Massacre*. Harcourt, 1993. Historical fiction.

North American Exploration

Harmon, David. *The Early French Explorers of North America.* Mason Crest Publishers, 2002.

Herbert, Janis. *Lewis and Clark for Kids*. Chicago Review Press, 2000. Great activity book that's filled
with information.

Karwoski, Gail L. *Seaman: The Dog Who Explored the West with Lewis & Clark*. Peachtree, 1999.
Historical fiction. The story of Lewis and Clark through the eyes of the Newfoundland dog.

Lewis, Meriwether, and William Clark. *The Journals of Lewis and Clark*. Ed. John Bakeless. New York:
Penguin Group, 2002.

O'Dell, Scott. *Carolta*. Laurel Leaf, 2006. Historical fiction. The story of a tomboy living in California in
1846 during the Spanish/American wars and the Gold Rush.

—*Streams to the River, River to the Sea*. Houghton Mifflin, 1986. Historical fiction. Lewis and Clark
from Sacagawea's perspective.

General and Other

Bauer, Susan Wise. *The Story of the World, Volume 3: Early Modern Times.* Peace Hill Press, 2004.

Paterson, Katherine. *The Puppeteer*. HarperTeen, 1989. Historical fiction. A young boy suffers through
poverty in 18th-century Japan.

Roth, Arthur. *The Iceberg Hermit*. Scholastic, 1989. Historical fiction. A 17-year-old boy must learn to survive after being shipwrecked in 1757 on an iceberg in the Arctic seas with only an orphaned polar cub for companionship. This book could be used for the compare and contrast survival stories assignment.

Thaceray, Frank W., and John E. Findling, eds. *Events That Changed the World in the 18th Century*. Greenwood, 1998.

Westwell, Ian. *Warfare in the 18th Century*. Raintree Steck-Vaughn, 1998.

Von Canon, Claudia. *The Moonclock*. Houghton, 1979. Historical fiction. Through a series of two letters couples relive their adventuress during the Turkish invasion of Austria in the 17th century.

Writing and Grammar

Finley, Robin. *Teaching the Essay*. www.analyticalgrammar.com. A short course on how to write a five-paragraph literary essay using *The Tell-Tale Heart* by Edgar Allan Poe and other short stories.

Gibaldi, Joseph. *MLA Handbook for Writers of Research Papers*. 6th ed. New York: The Modern Language Association of America, 2003.

Lutz, Gary and Diane Stevenson. *The Writer's Digest Grammar Desk Reference*. Writer's Digest Books: Cincinnati, 2005.

Teaching Writing, Structure & Style. Atascadero, California: The Institute for Excellence in Writing, 2001.

Writing Strands, Challenging Writing Projects for Homeschoolers. Niles, Michigan: National Writing Institute, 1995.

History Odyssey
Early Modern (level two)

Contents:

Record of War or Conflict (17)

Evaluating Sources in History (12)

Essay Worksheet (3)

Essay Rubric Checklist (3)

Trade and Rebellion Around the World

Revolution (5)

Agricultural Revolution Web

Industrial Revolution Web

Book Jacket Templates

Storyboard

The Enlightenment

Brochure Template

Causes of the American Revolution

"The Way to Wealth" Maxim Meanings

A Timeline of Slavery

Character Comparison Chart

Character Comparison Venn Diagram

Revolution Around the World

Timeline Analysis

(indicates number of copies needed for the course)

Record of War or Conflict

War or Conflict: [   ] Dates: [   ]

General Summary:

Parties Involved:

Events Leading Up to the War or Conflict:

Map Sketch

Reasons For the Fighting (Causes):

Significant Battles and Their Outcomes:

Final Outcome:

Results (Future Effects):

Other Information and Your Assessment:

Evaluating Sources in History

Title of the Work:

Type:

Author of the Work:

Date of the Work:

Subject of the Work:

☐ Primary Source
☐ Secondary Source

Intended Audience:

Purpose:

Summary:

Reliability/Validity:

Essay Worksheet

Topic

Topic Sentence

Main Idea	Main Idea	Main Idea

Introduction Paragraph (create from topic sentence and main ideas)

Body Paragraph 1 (create from main idea 1)

Body Paragraph 2 (create from main idea 2)

Body Paragraph 3 (create from main idea 3)

Conclusion paragraph

Essay Rubric Checklist

Essay Title: _____

Date: _____ Student: _____

Criteria	✓	Notes
Introduction catches reader's attention		
Introduction begins or ends with the topic sentence		
Topic sentence is detailed and expresses only one idea		
Each paragraph in the body begins with one main idea		
Body paragraphs contain examples that support the main idea		
Quotes are appropriately attributed		
Ideas taken from other works are rewritten in student's words		
Information is presented in a logical order		
Word choices are fresh and interesting		
Body paragraphs begin with transitional words		
Each paragraph contains five sentences or more		
Conclusion summarizes main ideas without restating exactly		
Grammar		
Spelling		
Punctuation		

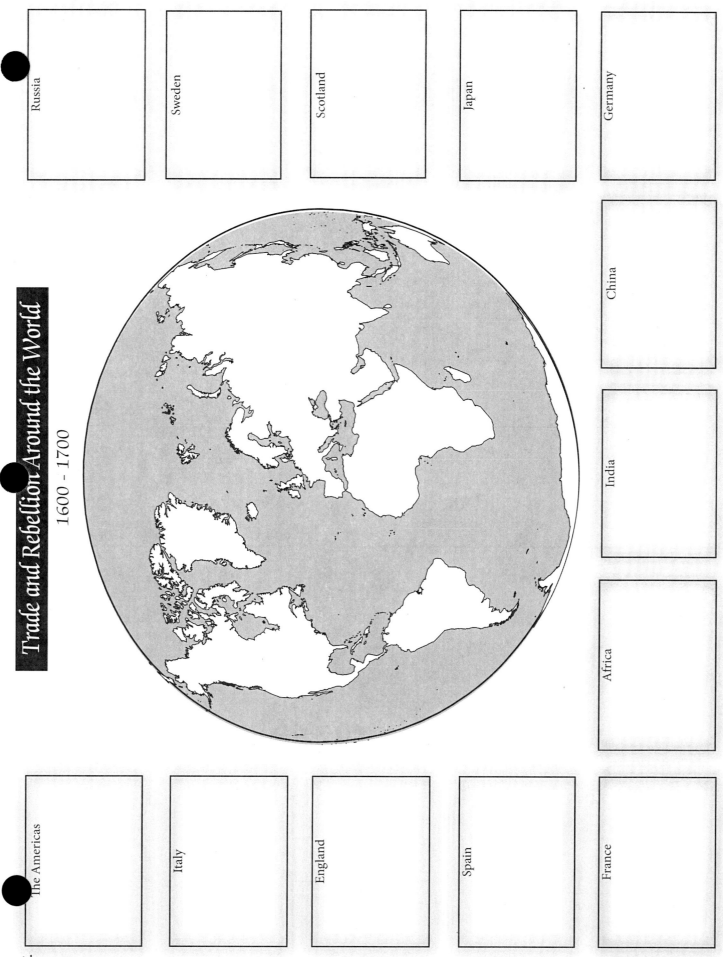

Trade and Rebellion Around the World
1600 - 1700

Russia

Sweden

Scotland

Japan

Germany

China

India

Africa

The Americas

Italy

England

Spain

France

THE _____ REVOLUTION

Dates: Place:

Definitions of *revolution*:

1.

2.

3.

Circumstances required for a revolution to take place:

1. Human rights are being violated.

2. The government is not meeting the demands of the people.

3. Most of the people want freedom or a change.

4. The people put aside their differences and unite to bring about change.

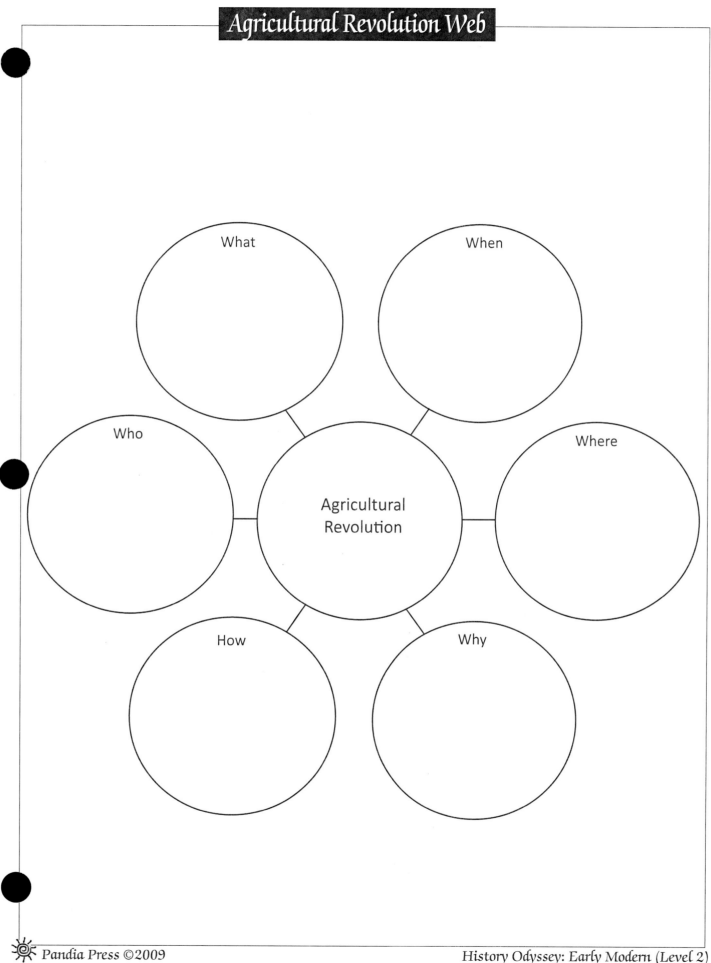

What

When

Who

Industrial
Revolution

Where

How

Why

Book Jacket Templates

(page one)

Front Cover

Spine

Front Inside Flap

Back Cover

Back Inside Flap

Storyboard

Title _____

Storyboard

DATES: _____   PLACE: _____

Knowledge

Justice

Science

Philosophy

Arts

Freedom & Liberty

BROCHURE TEMPLATE

fold line

fold line

Causes of the American Revolution

Event/Person/ Situation	Description	Effect	Rating ★ ★ ★ ★

"The Way to Wealth" Maxim Meanings

Maxim	Meaning
A word to the wise is enough.	
The used key is always bright.	
He that riseth late must trot all day.	
The eye of a master will do more work than both his hands.	
Many estate are spent in the getting.	
Many a little makes a mickle.	
Experience keeps a dear school, but fools will learn in no other.	
What maintains one vice would bring up two children.	
If you will not hear Reason, she will surely rap your knuckles.	
Pride is as loud a beggar as Want, and a great deal more saucy.	
Vessels large may venture more, But little boats should keep near shore.	
(Your favorite maxim)	

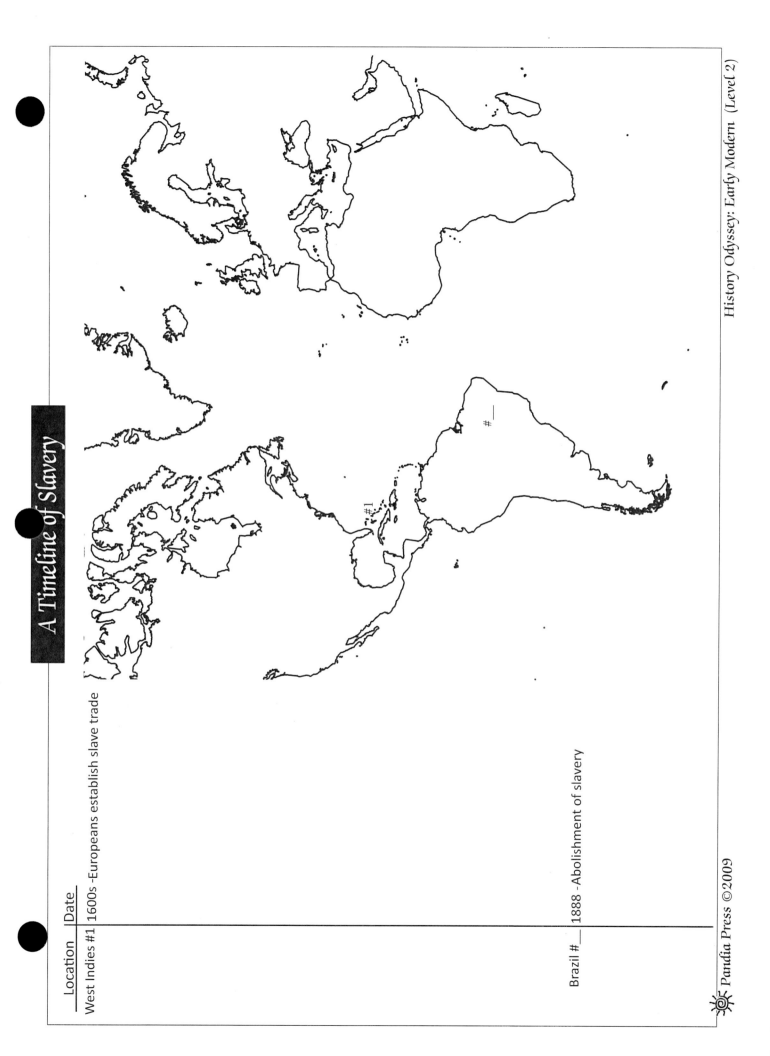

A Timeline of Slavery

Location	Date
West Indies #1	1600s - Europeans establish slave trade
Brazil #___	1888 - Abolishment of slavery

#1

#___

Character Comparison Chart

	Karana *The Island of the Blue Dolphins*	Matt *The Sign of the Beaver*	Crusoe *Robinson Crusoe*
Location			
Survival skills and knowledge			
Character growth and changes			
Feelings and coping strategies (e.g. loneliness)			
Tragedies			
Courage and strength			
Length of isolation			
Help received, company, friends			
Weapons			
Enemies			
Food			
Shelter			
Rescue			

Pandia Press ©2009

Character Comparison Venn Diagram

Matt

Karana

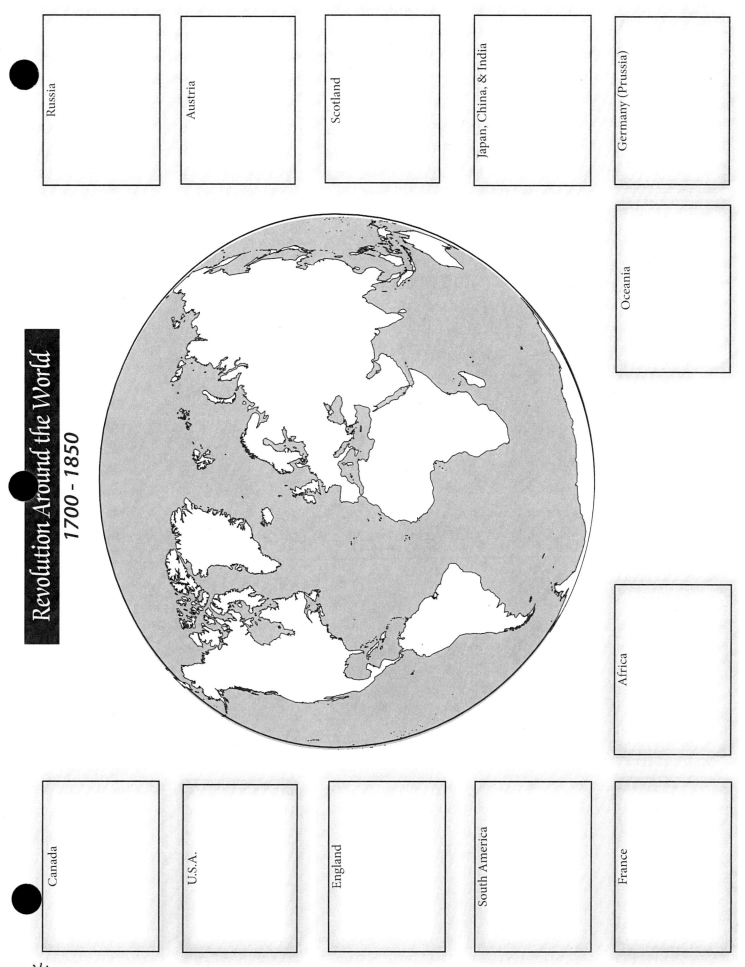

Revolution Around the World
1700 - 1850

Russia

Austria

Scotland

Japan, China, & India

Germany (Prussia)

Oceania

Africa

Canada

U.S.A.

England

South America

France

Timeline Analysis page 1

Area / Date range	North America	South America	Africa	Europe	Asia	Oceania
1600 - 1625						
1626 - 1650						
1651 - 1675						
1676 - 1700						
1701 - 1725						
1726 - 1750						

Timeline Analysis page 2

Area Date range	North America	South America	Africa	Europe	Asia	Oceania
1751 - 1775						
1776 - 1800						
1801 - 1825						
1826 - 1850						
1851 +						

HISTORY ODYSSEY
EARLY MODERN (LEVEL TWO)

Below is a list of the maps included with this course. You might want to make extra copies of the maps, saving the original.

Map 1: 17th Century Europe

Map 2: The Thirty Years' War (1648)

Map 3: 17th Century France

Map 4: Spain

Map 5: Early North American Settlements

Map 6: India

Map 7: East India Trading Companies

Map 8: Africa and the Slave Trade, 16th to 19th Centuries

Map 9: 17th and 18th Century Japan

Map 10: Qing Dynasty in China

Map 11: Colonial America

Map 12: 18th Century Russia

Map 13: Swedish Empire 1660

Map 14: Great Britain, 18th Century

Map 15: The Seven Years' War (Europe)

Map 16: Seven Years' War (North America)

Map 17: The Voyages of Nathaniel Bowditch

Map 18: The French Empire Under Napoleon (1812)

Map 19: Latin America 1808 - 1830

Map 20: Oceania Discovered

Map 21: United States Territories

Map 1

17th Century Europe

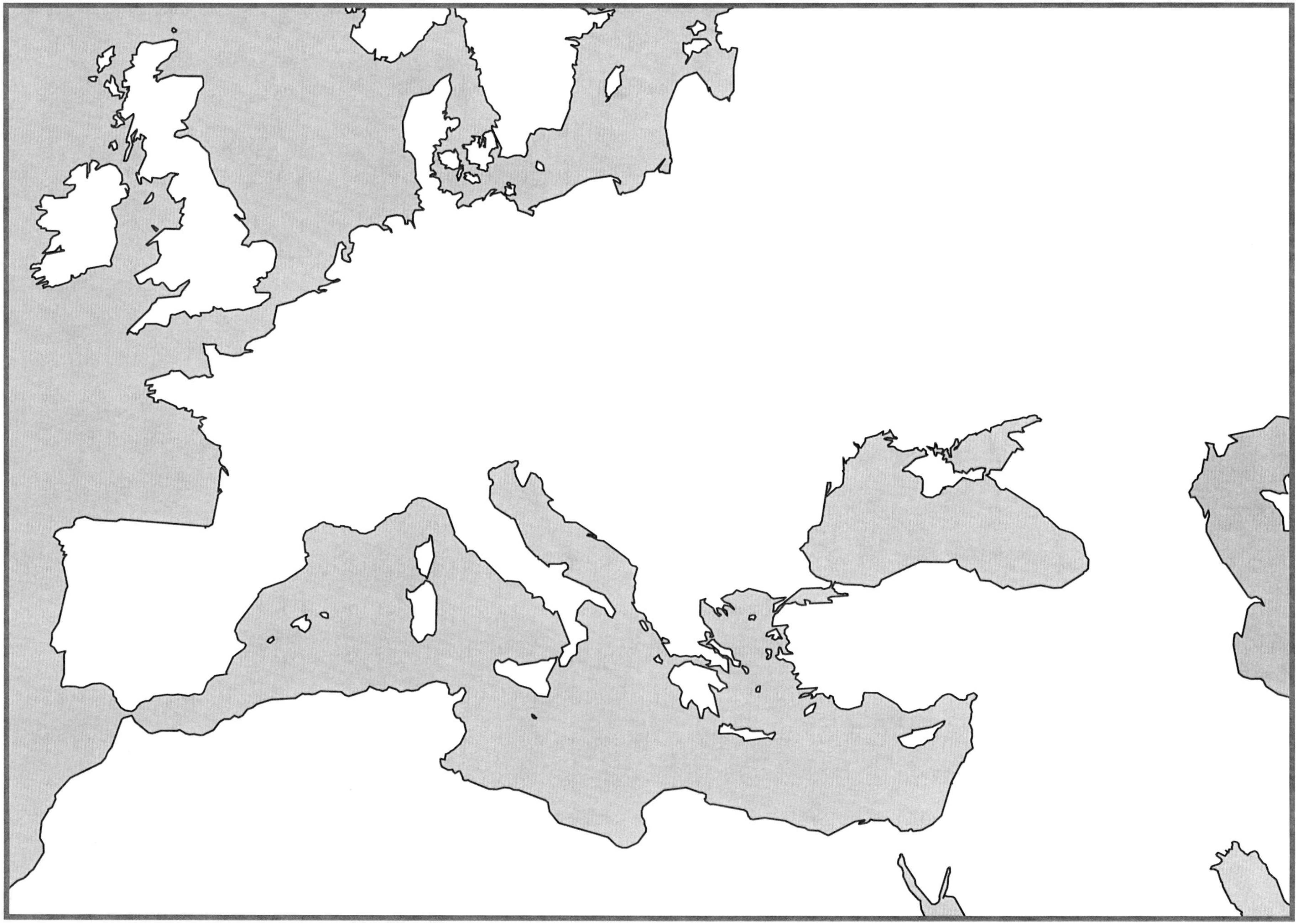

Map 2

The Thirty Years' War (1648)

PRUSSIA

BRANDENBURG-PRUSSIA

BOHEMIA

BAVARIA

Map 3

17th Century France

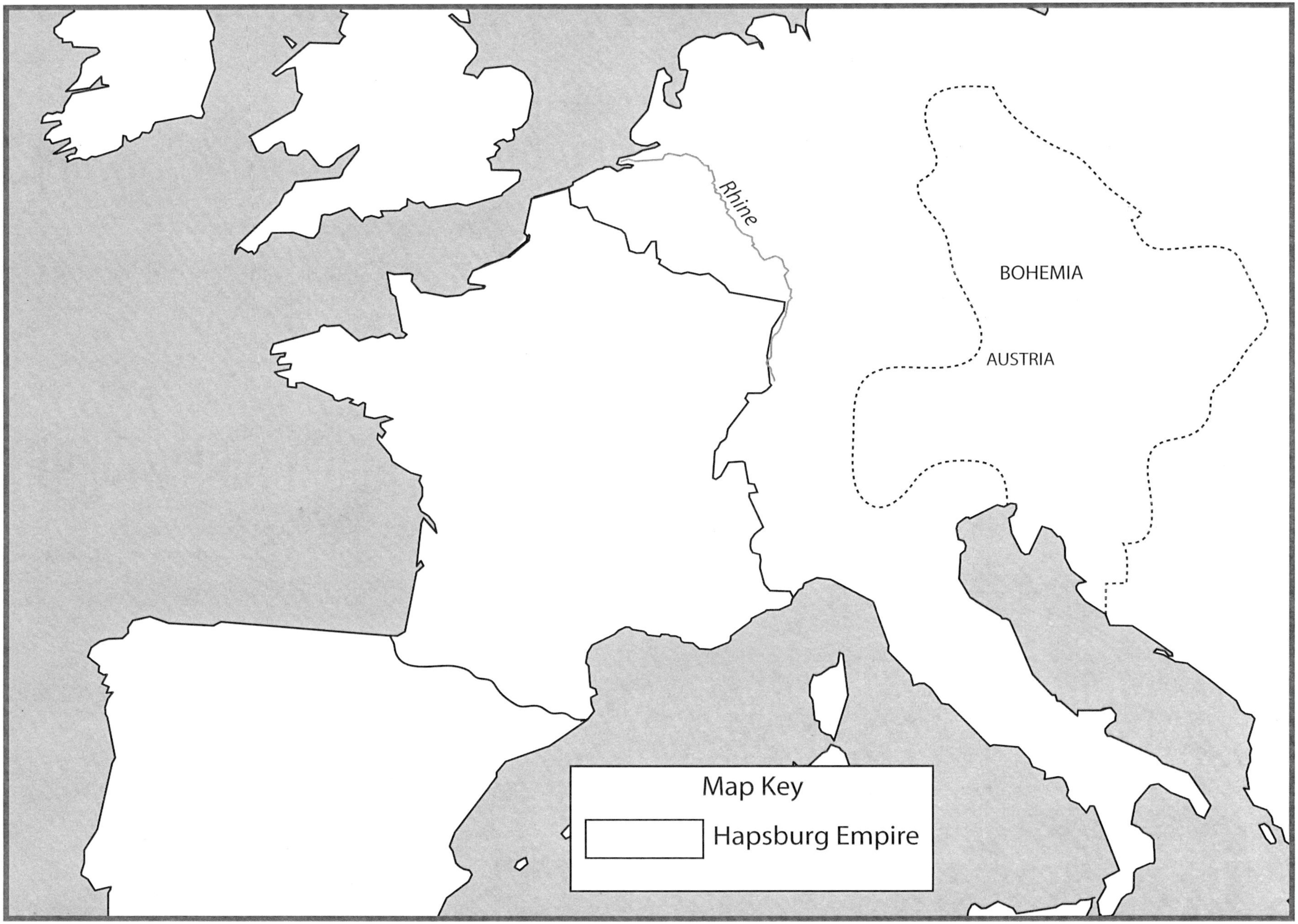

BOHEMIA

AUSTRIA

Rhine

Map Key

Hapsburg Empire

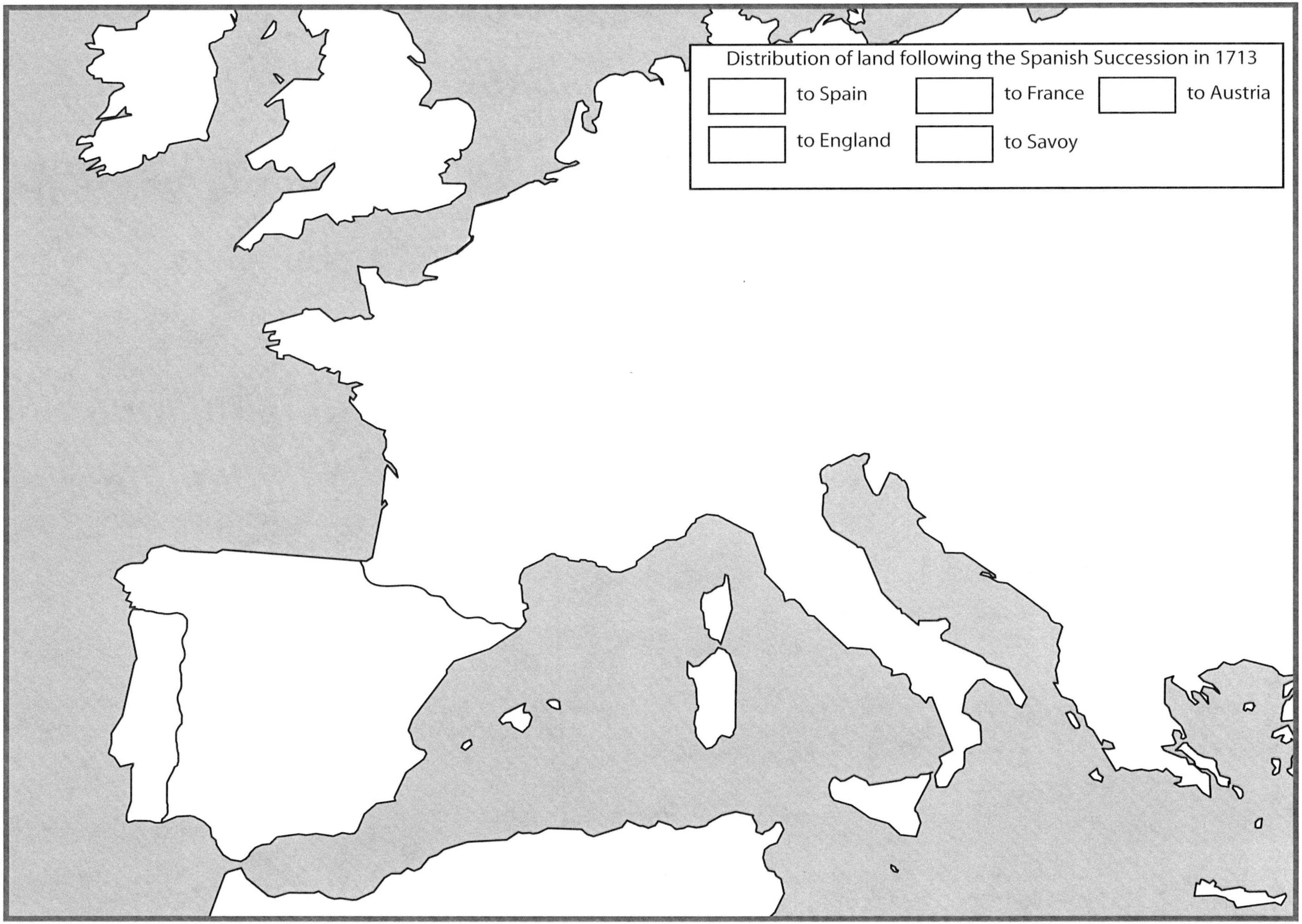

Map 4

Spain

Distribution of land following the Spanish Succession in 1713

to Spain

to France

to Austria

to England

to Savoy

Map 5

Early North American Settlements

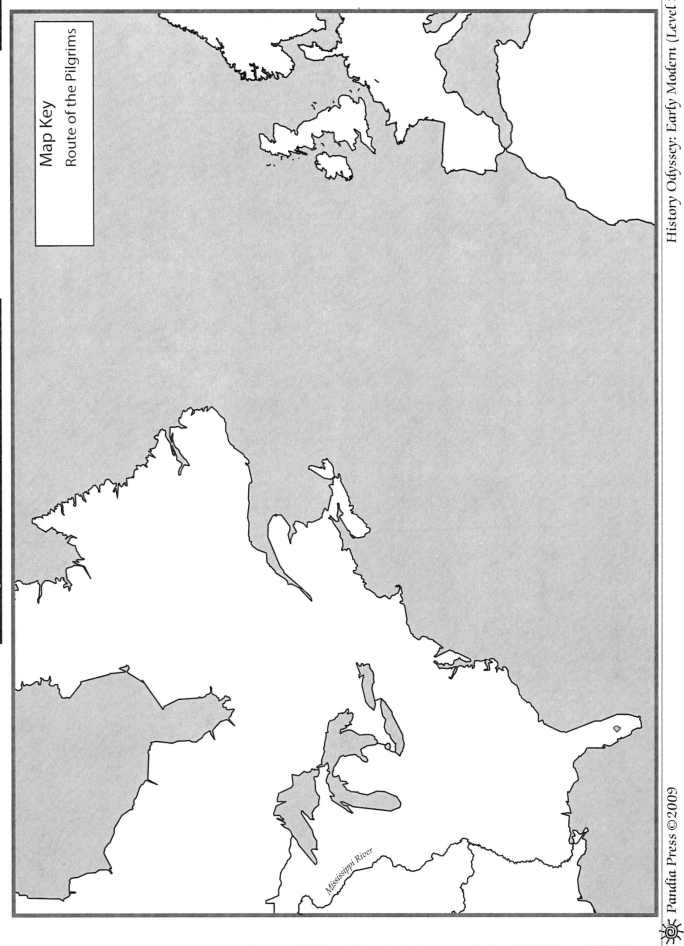

Map Key

Route of the Pilgrims

Mississippi River

Map 6

India

Ganges River

Yamuna River

●Agra

Indus River

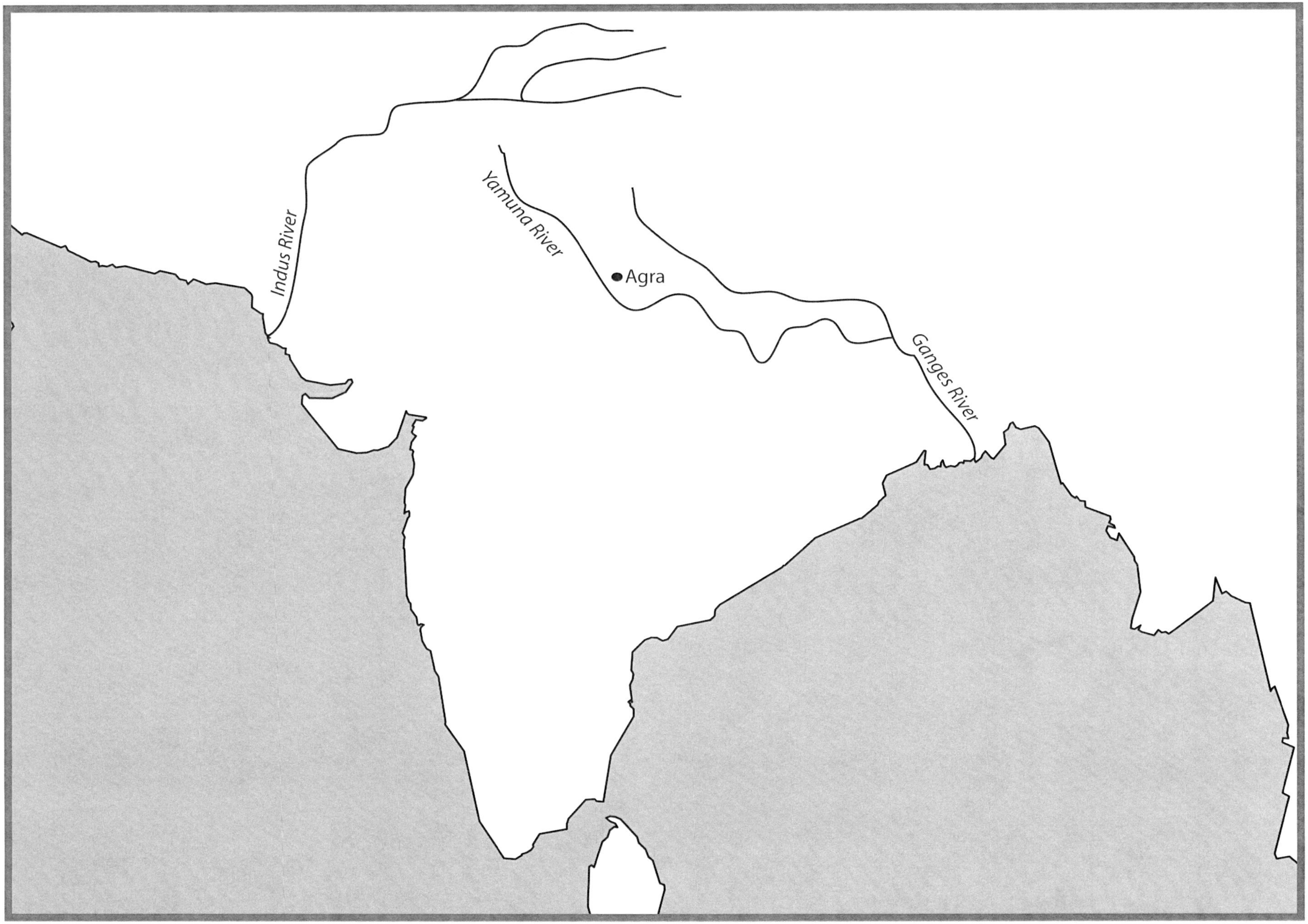

Map 7

East India Trading Companies

PERSIA

Calcutta

Madras
(Chennai)

Ceylon
(Sri Lanka)

Java

Cape of
Good Hope

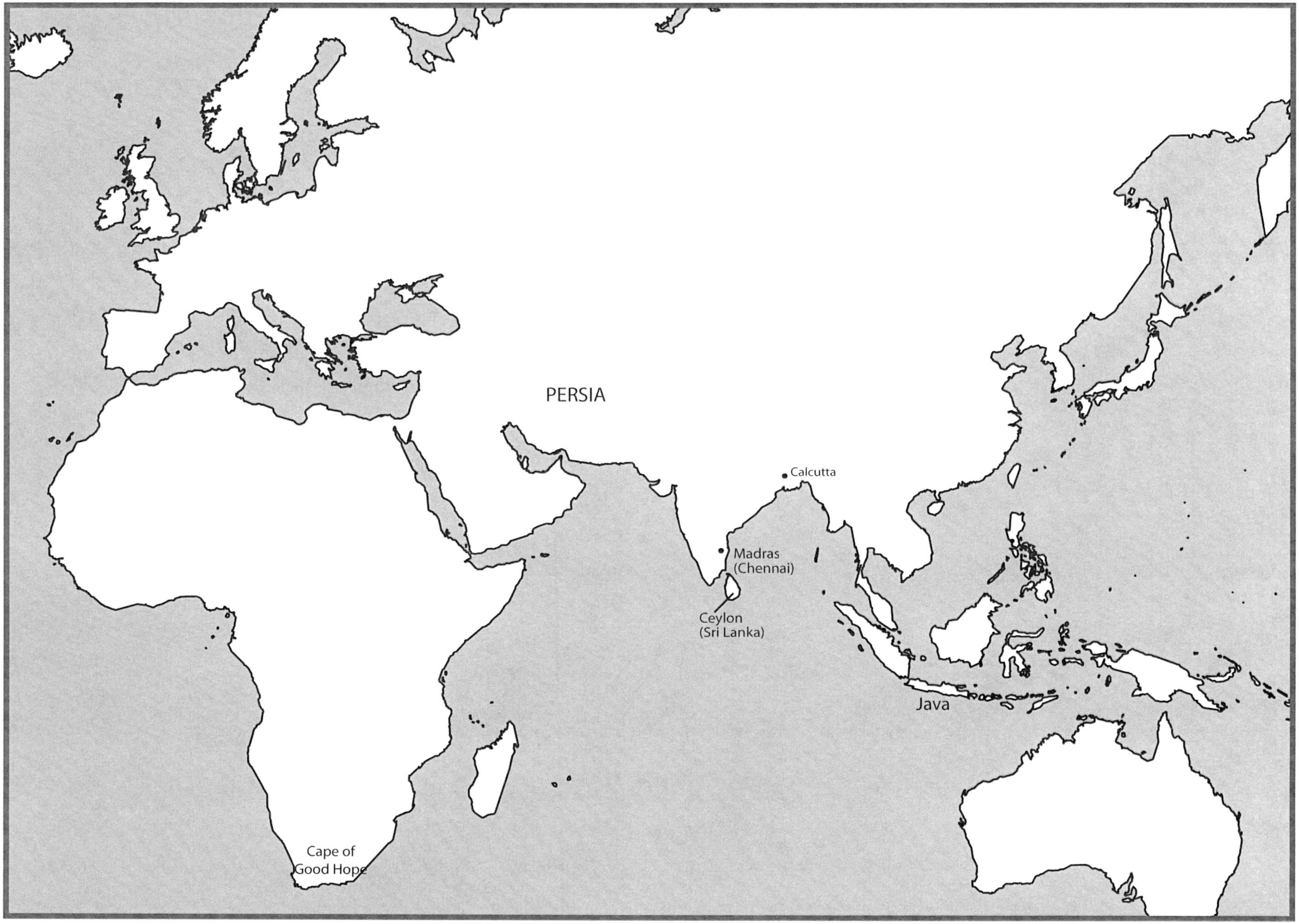

Map 8

Africa and the Slave Trade, 16th to 19th Centuries

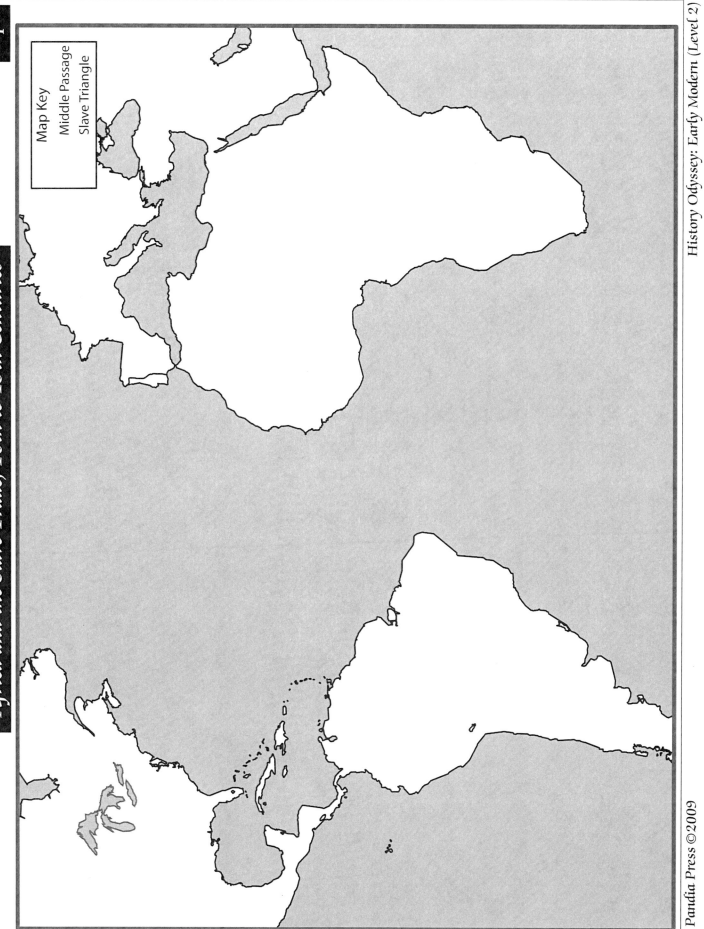

Map Key
Middle Passage
Slave Triangle

Map 9

17th and 18th Century Japan

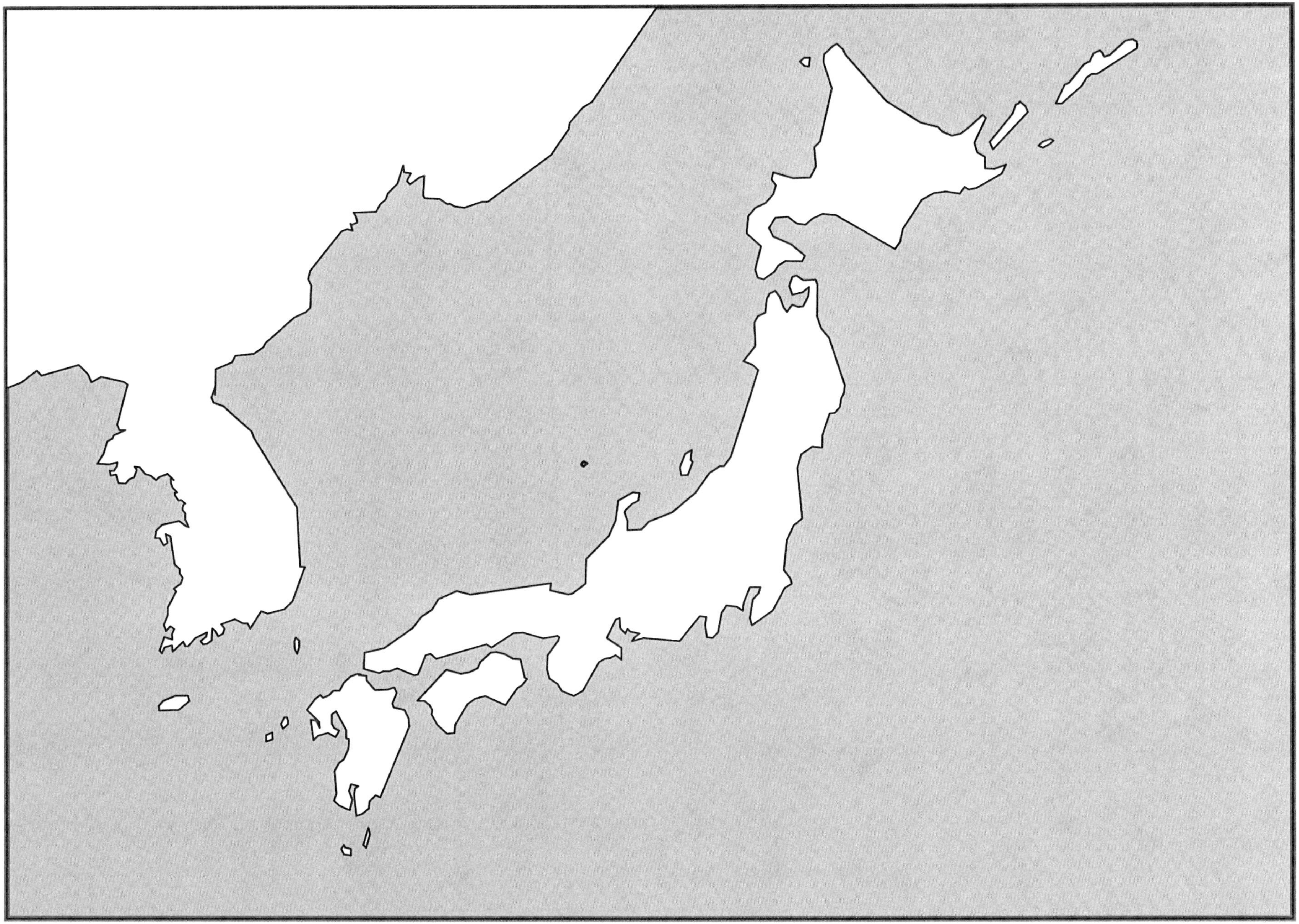

History Odyssey: Early Modern (Level 2)

map 10

Qing Dynasty in China

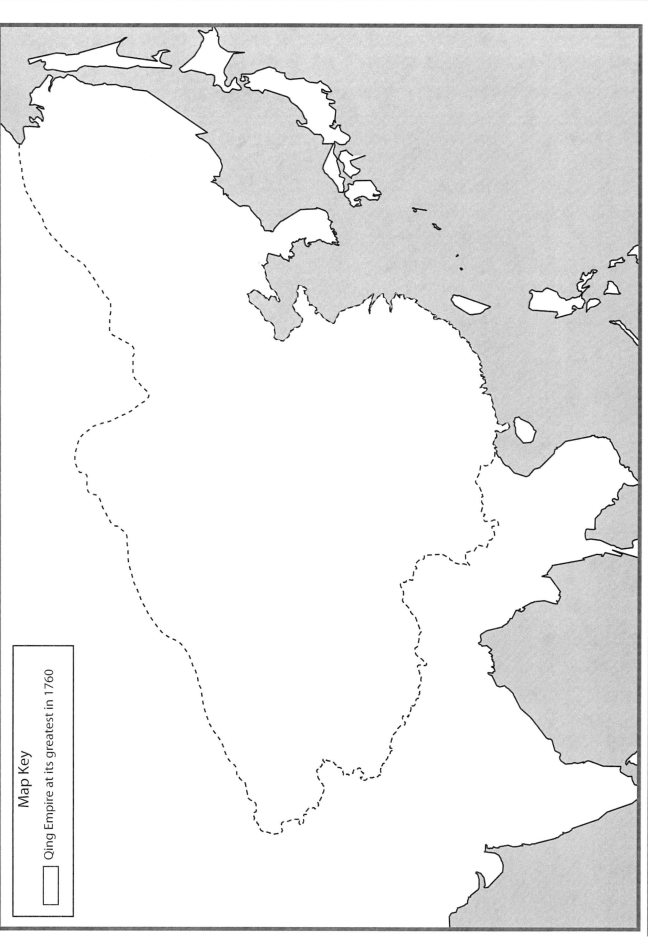

Map Key

Qing Empire at its greatest in 1760

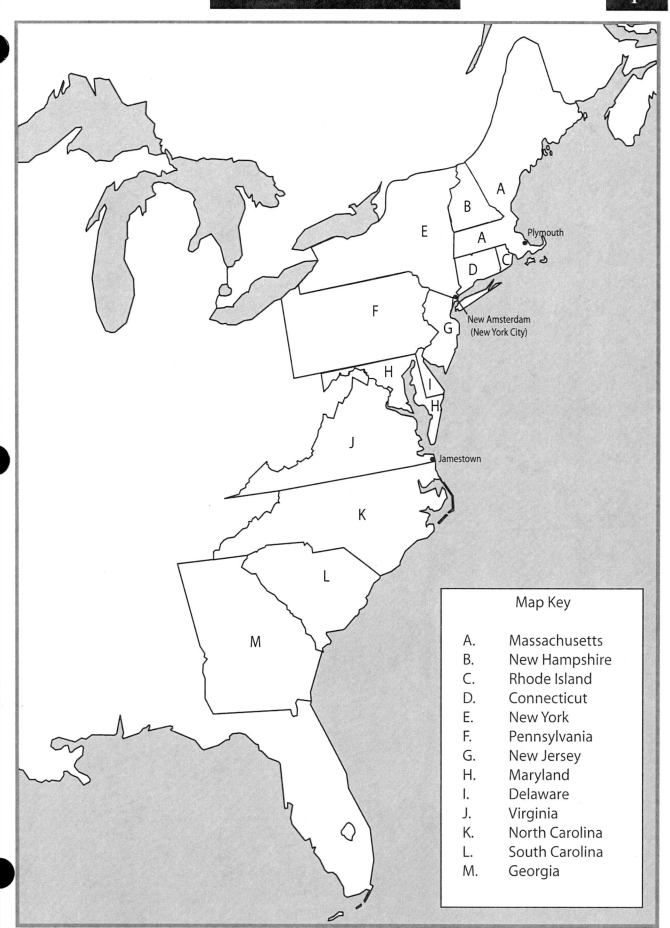

Plymouth

New Amsterdam
(New York City)

Jamestown

Map Key

A.   Massachusetts
B.   New Hampshire
C.   Rhode Island
D.   Connecticut
E.   New York
F.   Pennsylvania
G.   New Jersey
H.   Maryland
I.   Delaware
J.   Virginia
K.   North Carolina
L.   South Carolina
M.   Georgia

Map 12

18th Century Russia

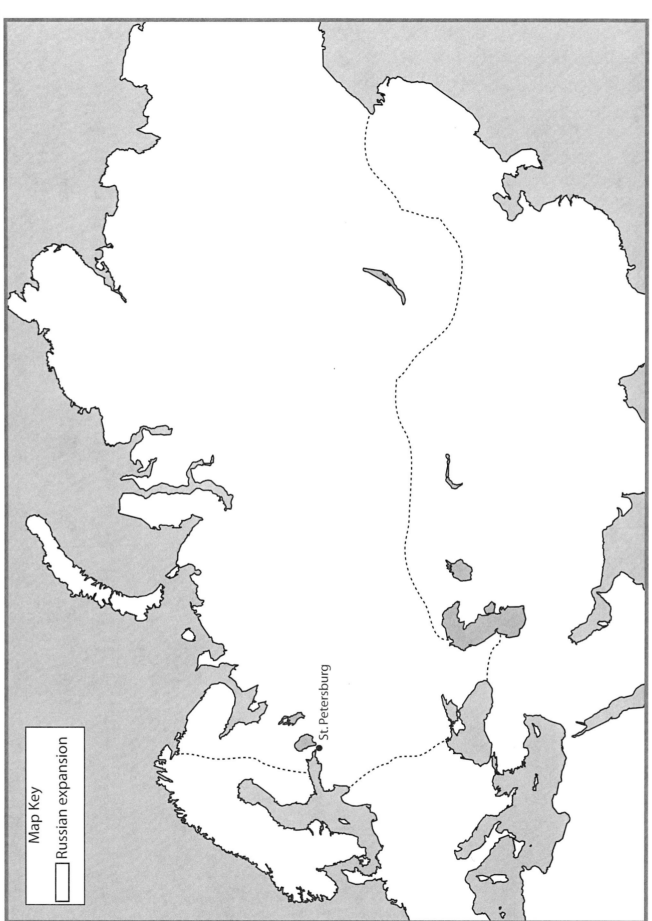

Map Key

Russian expansion

St. Petersburg

History Odyssey: Early Modern (Level 2)

Map 13

Swedish Empire 1660

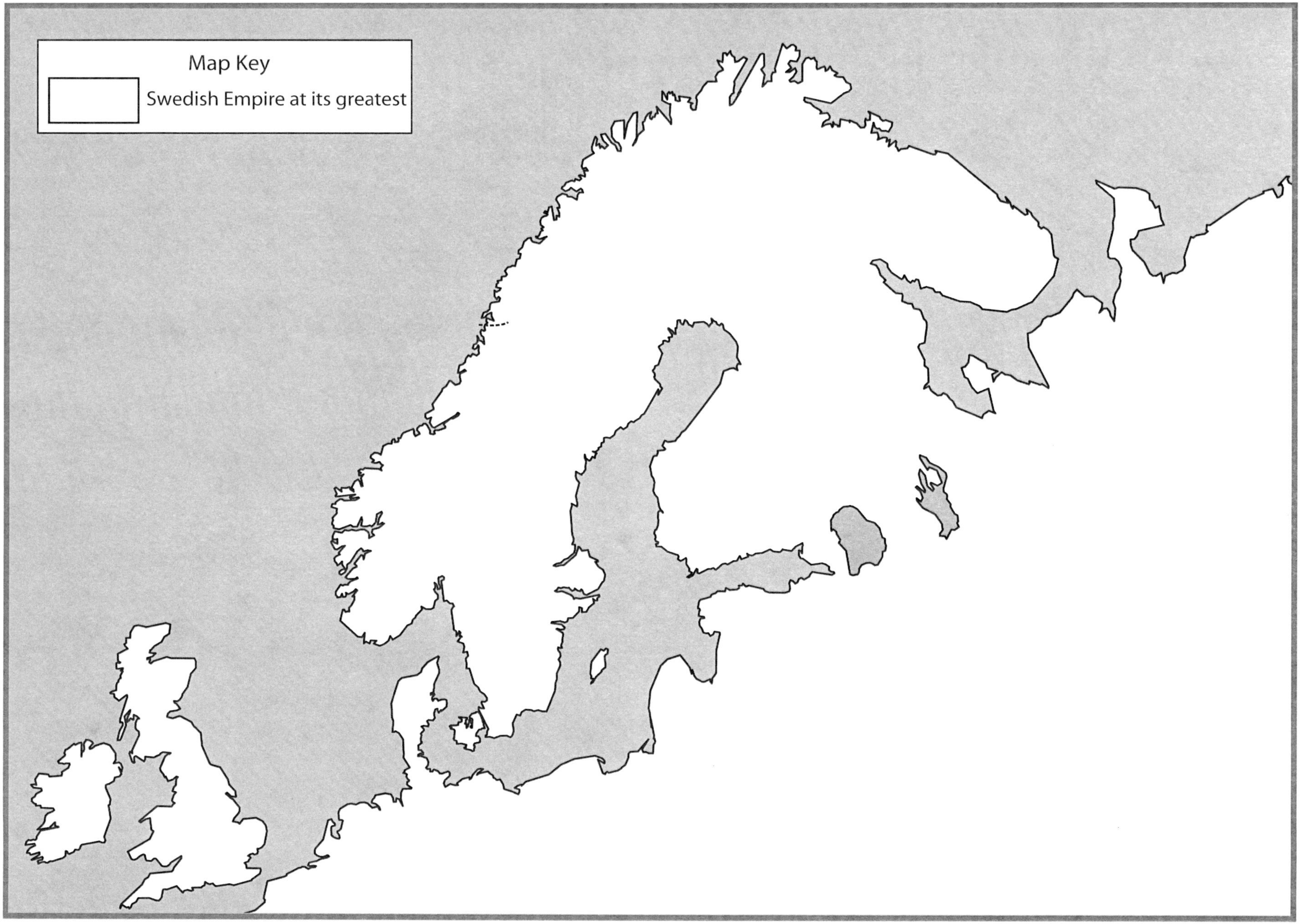

Map Key

Swedish Empire at its greatest

Map 15

The Seven Years' War (Europe)

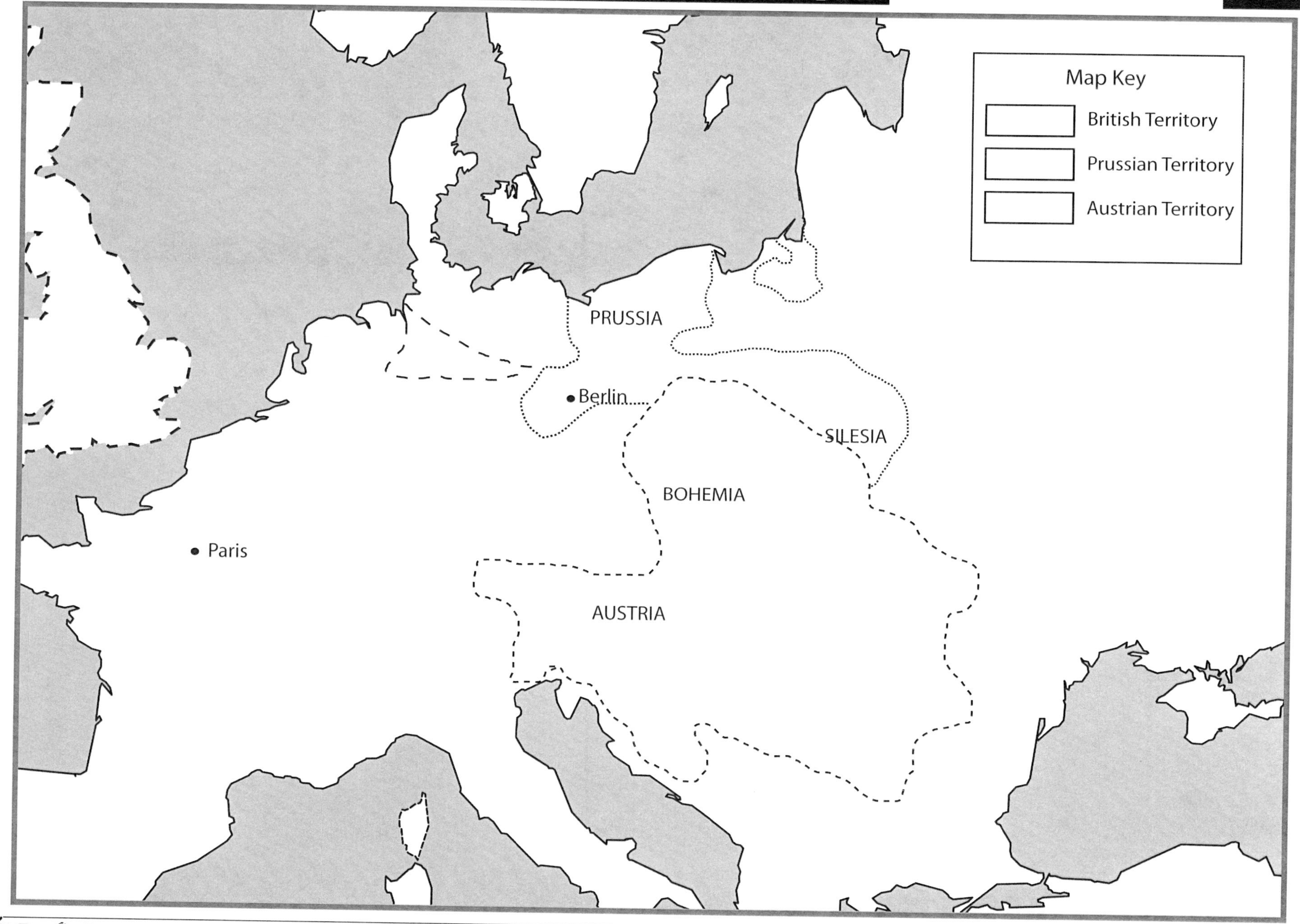

Map Key

☐ British Territory

☐ Prussian Territory

☐ Austrian Territory

PRUSSIA

Berlin

SILESIA

BOHEMIA

AUSTRIA

Paris

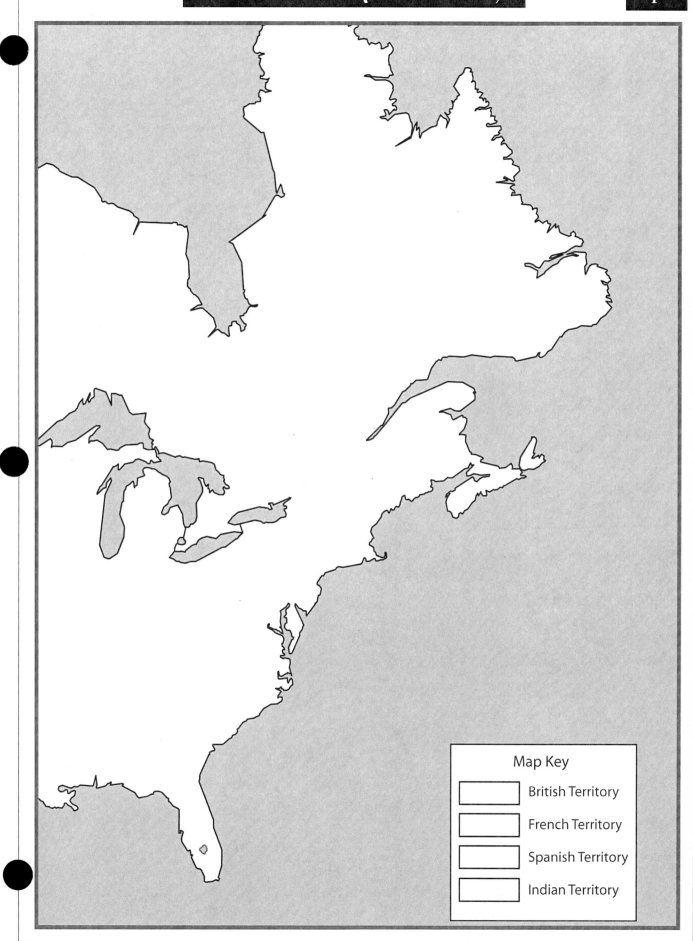

Map Key

British Territory

French Territory

Spanish Territory

Indian Territory

Map 17

The Voyages of Nathaniel Bowditch

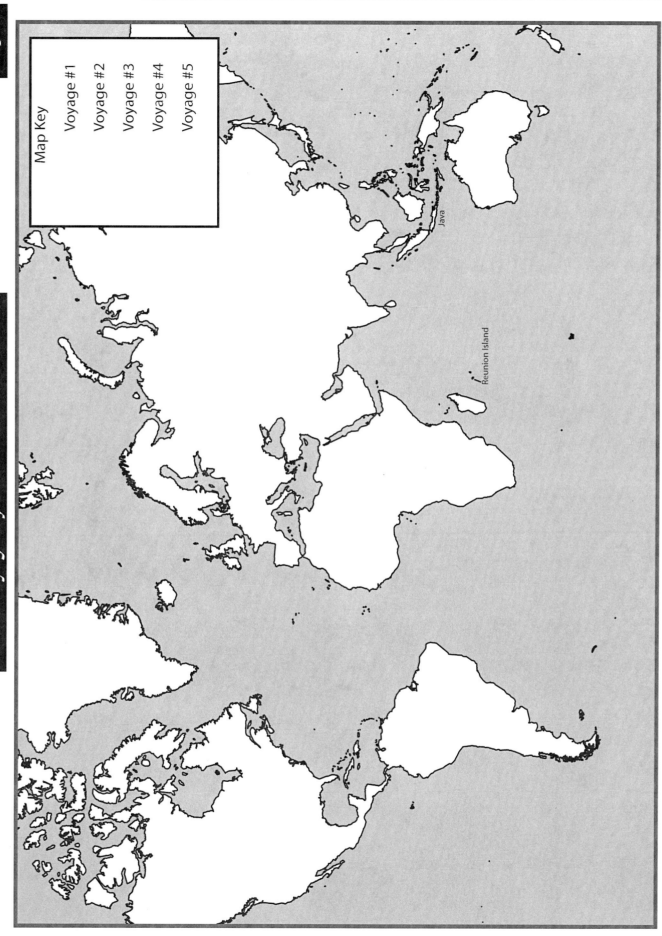

Map Key

Voyage #1
Voyage #2
Voyage #3
Voyage #4
Voyage #5

Java

Reunion Island

map 18

The French Empire Under Napoleon (1812)

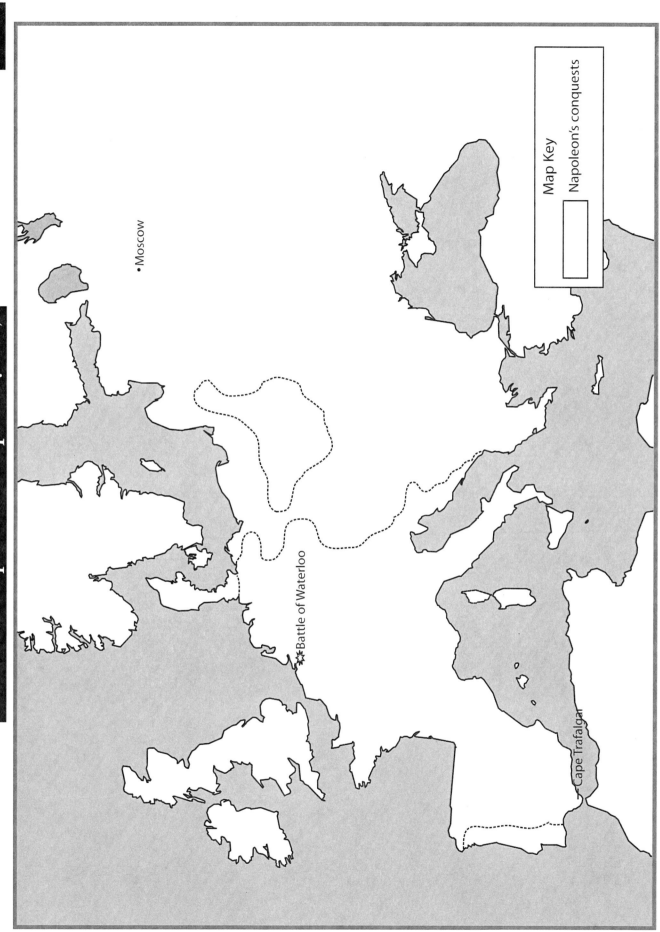

Map Key

Napoleon's conquests

• Moscow

Battle of Waterloo

Cape Trafalgar

Map 19

Latin America 1808 - 1830

Map 20

Oceania

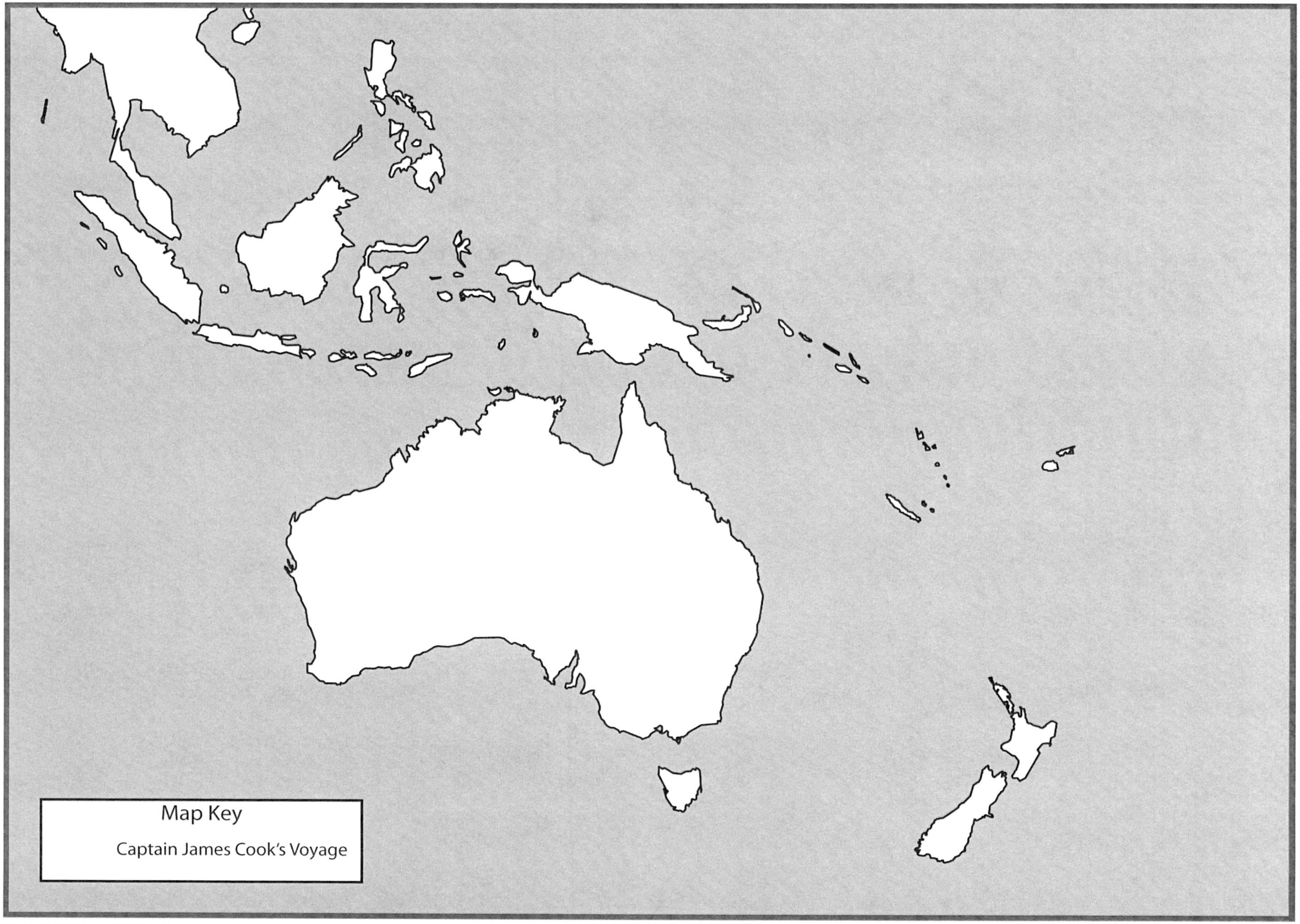

Map Key
Captain James Cook's Voyage

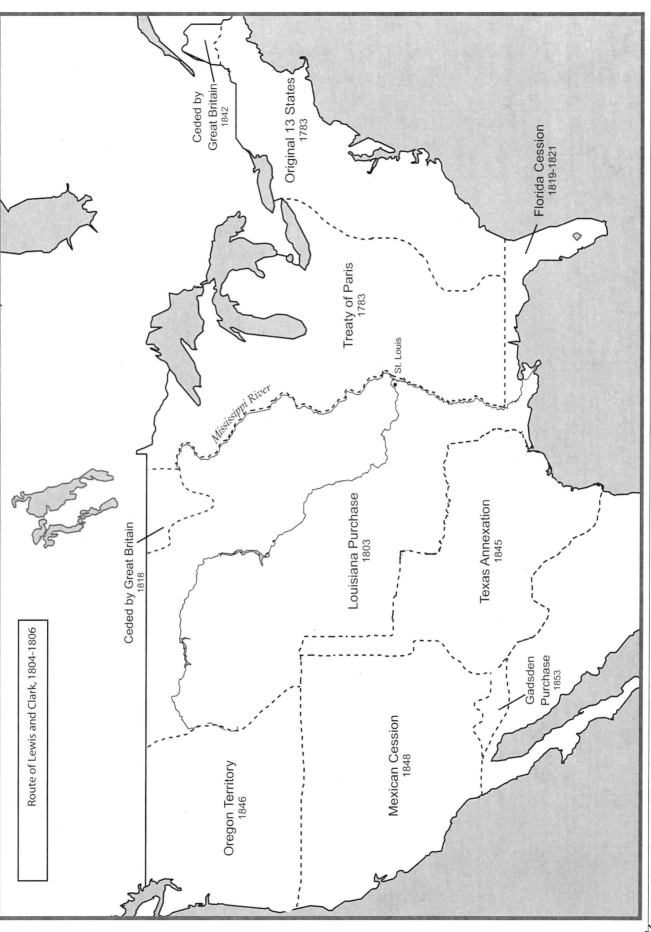

Map 21

United States Territories

Route of Lewis and Clark, 1804-1806

Ceded by Great Britain 1818

Ceded by Great Britain 1842

Original 13 States 1783

Florida Cession 1819-1821

Treaty of Paris 1783

Mississippi River

St. Louis

Oregon Territory 1846

Louisiana Purchase 1803

Texas Annexation 1845

Mexican Cession 1848

Gadsden Purchase 1853